Spooky Britain

CONWAY
Bloomsbury Publishing Plc
50 Bedford Square, London, WC1B 3DP, UK
Bloomsbury Publishing Ireland Limited,
29 Earlsfort Terrace, Dublin 2, D02 AY28,
Ireland

BLOOMSBURY, CONWAY and the Conway logo are trademarks of Bloomsbury Publishing Plc

First published in Great Britain 2026

This book is a guide for when you spend time outdoors. Undertaking any activity outdoors carries with it some risks that cannot be entirely eliminated. For example, you might get lost on a route or caught in bad weather. Before you spend time outdoors, we therefore advise that you always take the necessary precautions, such as checking weather forecasts and ensuring that you have all the equipment you need. Any walking routes that are described in this book should not be relied upon as a sole means of navigation, so we recommend that you refer to an Ordnance Survey map or authoritative equivalent.

This book may also reference businesses and venues. Whilst every effort is made by the author and the publisher to ensure the accuracy of the business and venue information contained in our books before they go to print, changes to such information can occur during the production and lifetime of a publication. Therefore, we also advise that you check with businesses or venues for the latest information before setting out.

All internet addresses given in this book were correct at the time of going to press. Bloomsbury Publishing Plc does not have any control over, or responsibility for, any third-party websites referred to or in this book.

The author and the publisher regret any inconvenience caused if some facts have changed or sites have ceased to exist, but can accept no responsibility for any such changes.

A catalogue record for this book is available from the British Library

Library of Congress Cataloguing-in-Publication data has been applied for

ISBN: PB: 978-1-8448-6760-8; ePub: 978-1-8448-6761-5; ePDF: 978-1-8448-6758-5

10 9 8 7 6 5 4 3 2 1

Typeset in Silva Text
Designed by Austin Taylor
Printed and bound in China by Toppan Leefung

MIX
Paper | Supporting responsible forestry
FSC® C104723
www.fsc.org

To find out more about our authors and books visit www.bloomsbury.com and sign up for our newsletters
For product safety related questions contact productsafety@bloomsbury.com

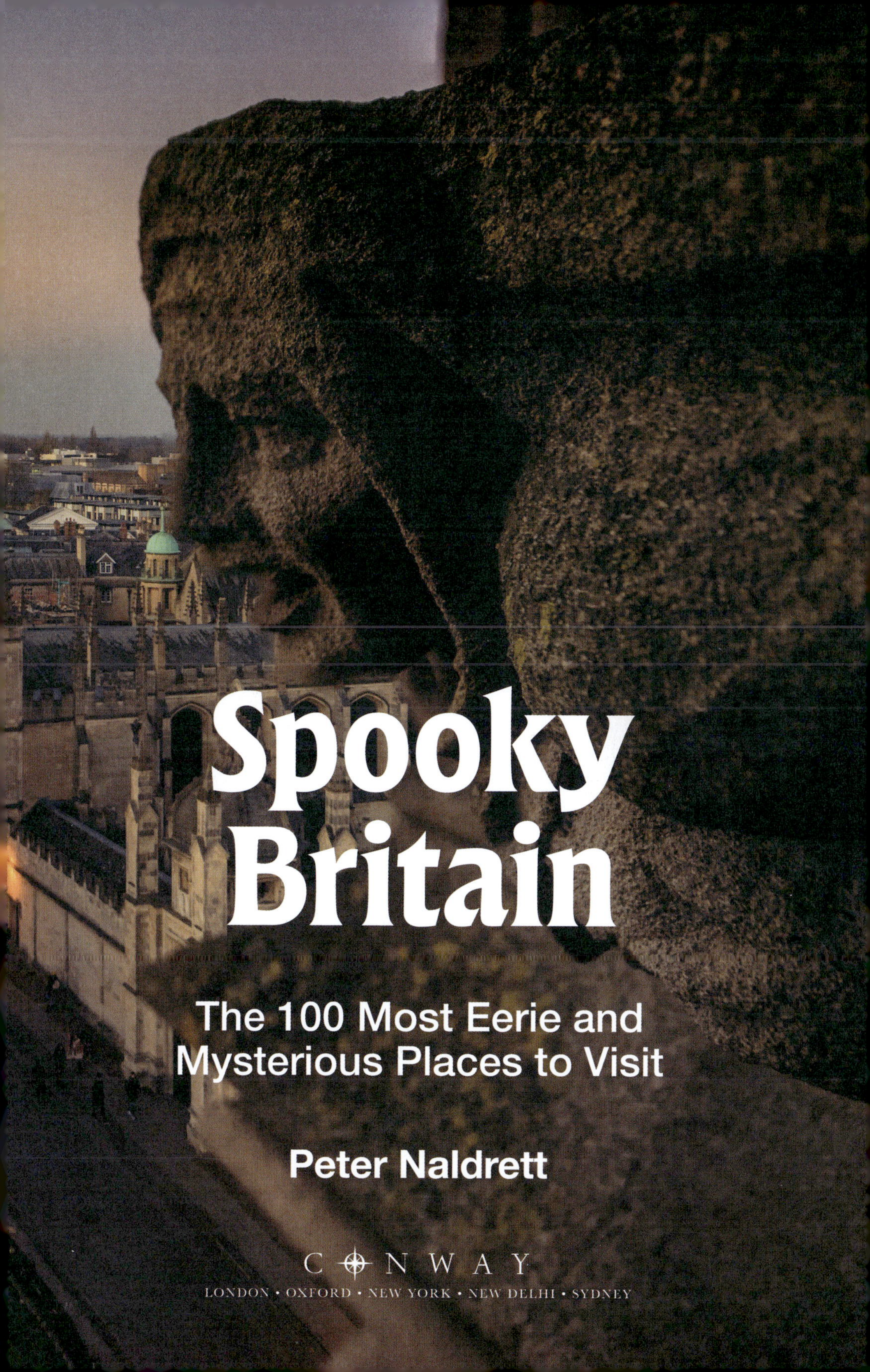

Spooky Britain

The 100 Most Eerie and Mysterious Places to Visit

Peter Naldrett

CONWAY
LONDON • OXFORD • NEW YORK • NEW DELHI • SYDNEY

Contents

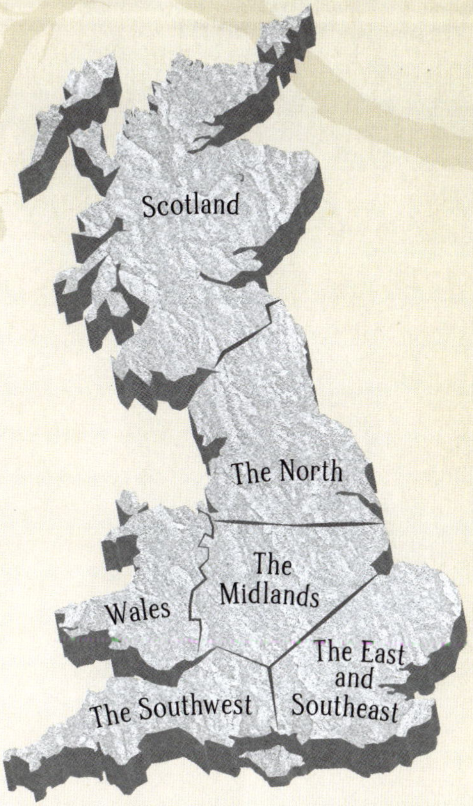
Scotland
The North
The Midlands
Wales
The East and Southeast
The Southwest

The North 110

Introduction

Many years ago, when all the cool kids were listening to *Automatic for the People* and watching *The X Files*, I am convinced I lived in a haunted house. That's not an easy thing for me to write. If I listen to Danny Robins' *Uncanny* podcast, I always put myself in the position of what he likes to call 'Team Cynic.' When I watch TV programmes about Bigfoot and poltergeists, about mysterious black dogs and whispering voices in the woods, I often shake my head with bewilderment.

Surely, none of it can be real. You see, I'm not a *natural* believer. I try to find a scientific explanation for ghostly stories. Back in the 1990s, I enjoyed a good ghost story or horror film, but I was not somebody who was actively looking to have a paranormal experience. But, my goodness, I certainly had one.

It was the second year at Lancaster University and I lived with three other people on Ullswater Road, close to the city centre. It was a regular terraced house. There were many other students living in similar properties close by. Over the first few weeks and months, there were a few strange things that raised eyebrows. Electrical items turned themselves on and off. A bottle top flew across the room. Nobody really thought any more about it. Certainly nobody thought about moving out. It was kind of funny at first. The type of thing you tell stories about in the JCR.

But soon after Christmas I noticed a black dust, a little like ash, appear on my pillow. Not every day, but more than once. It would be there when I came back from lectures from time to time, sitting in the imprint where my head had been. Once I ruled out dirt, dandruff and residual from the oh-so-90s wet-look hair gel, I started to worry about it. I remember trying to work out what it could be. The only possibility I could come up with was it was some soil in a plant pot that had somehow got onto the bed. But that plant pot – my singular, badly watered plant – was on the other side of the room. And anyway, how could it get over to the pillow on its own? It made no sense. But week by week, there continued to be the odd day when black dust settled on my pillow. I'd never made so many trips to the laundrette.

Then, one Sunday afternoon, I was working at my desk in front of the attic dormer window when this ash-like substance started to fall from above. I stood on my chair to see where it was coming from, but I found no source. And yet it continued to float down, literally appearing as coming out of mid-air. It wasn't coming from the ceiling, nor the window. But down it slowly floated, eventually landing on a letter I was writing to a friend at the time (remember the time before email and texts when you actually had to put pen to paper). Well, I smudged the ash around the paper and actually wrote that this was the ash I had told them about previously. A few weeks later, I heard that this 'falling ash' had been reported before in properties where there was a strong spiritual presence. It actually featured in an episode of *The X Files*. I can remember feeling bewildered when I watched that episode some weeks later.

Other incidents took place around the same time. One night while I was asleep, I saw the curtains open a little, allowing the glow from the streetlight to enter the room. And while in the house on my own, I very strongly felt a presence move up the stairs and wait outside the door of my bedroom. This event terrified me. But I was a student and didn't have the financial option of moving to new digs. I had to stay on Ullswater Road. However, from that moment on I made sure I did not go through the property's red door unless at least one of my housemates was already inside.

Almost as fascinating as the events themselves were the reactions of people I knew. As soon as I had a genuine spooky story, everybody wanted to hear it and I was constantly asked for updates. There's a strange, curious fascination with tales of the paranormal. TV programmes dealing with the subject keep pulling in good viewer numbers, plays in the West End featuring ghostly goings-on sell out nightly and the more recent podcast phenomenon sees millions of followers get updated on paranormal events every week.

As a travel writer, I've been to many places that have claimed to have a spooky backstory. When you compile all the castles, museums, pubs, battlefields and city centres that have haunting, chilling and creepy stories linked to them, you begin to realise just how much of a spooky place the UK is. There are thousands upon thousands of dark yet intriguing stories on these shores, from witchcraft and wizardry to ghostly sightings and rumours of strange beasts. Too many stories, some would say, for them all to be dismissed as nonsense. And so in this book I go out in search of the spooky, the ghostly, the mysterious and the eerie – not just to paint a picture of our paranormal heritage but also to help you get out there and explore these strange occurrences for yourself. Some are genuinely scary, some are just good old fun. There are haunted pubs with curses, and dungeons where actors will give you a scare talking about body snatchers. There are terrifying nights spent in haunted houses, and

family-friendly ghost walks around ancient city centres. There are rumours of dead soldiers walking on the site of a ferocious historic battle, and a gloriously entertaining evening to be had on a decked-out ghost bus.

Time has passed since the events on Ullswater Road brought shivers to my spine and, thankfully, I've not experienced anything like that since. As the years go by, I find myself drifting away from being a believer and stepping into my old, cynical ways, trying to explain things scientifically. Was it even true? Did it even happen? Don't I just sound like one of those people on the TV who either likes making things up for attention or is actually certified bonkers? But no, it was something I experienced. And so when I do hear somebody describing their seemingly impossible stories with a convincing passion, there's always a lingering thought in the back of my mind: What if they are telling the truth? What if those things really happened?

Make your own spooky adventures make you smile. And shiver.

Key to symbols

- MUSEUMS
- GHOSTS
- WALKS AND TOURS
- CRIME AND PUNISHMENT
- CHURCHES AND RELIGIOUS SITES
- WITCHES
- ANCIENT SITES
- PUBS
- COUNTRYSIDE AND NATURE
- CASTLES AND HALLS
- BURIAL SITES
- THEATRES
- HISTORICAL SITES
- VAMPIRES AND OTHER MONSTERS
- PARKS AND GARDENS

01 **Museum of Witchcraft and Magic,** Boscastle, Cornwall
02 **Charlotte Dymond Memorial,** Roughtor, Cornwall
03 **Bodmin Jail,** Cornwall
04 **Buckland Abbey,** nr Yelverton, Devon
05 **Tyneham Village,** Wareham, Dorset
06 **Dorchester Prison,** Dorset
07 **Glastonbury Tor,** Somerset
08 **Shepton Mallet Prison,** Somerset
09 **Gough's Cave,** Cheddar Gorge, Somerset
10 **The Ancient Ram Inn,** Wotton-under-Edge, Gloucestershire
11 **Avebury Stone Circle,** Marlborough, Wiltshire

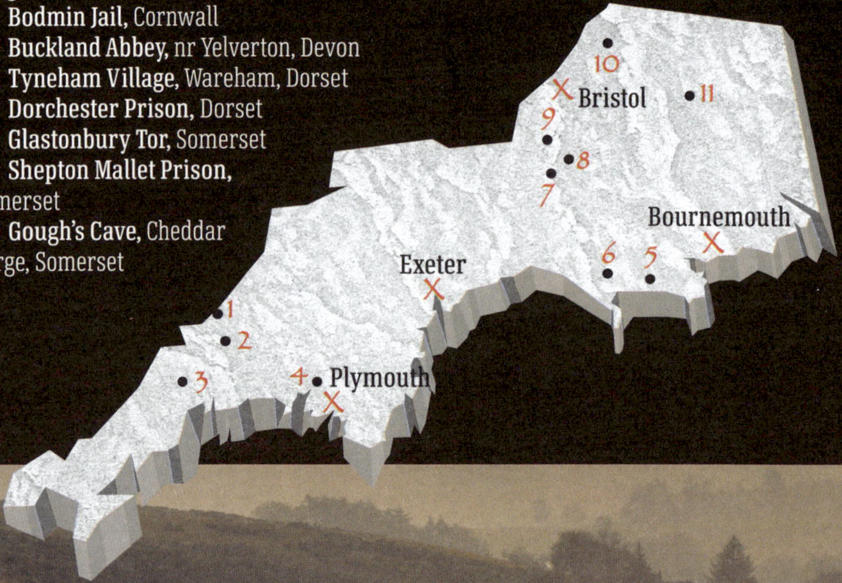

The Southwest

01 Museum of Witchcraft and Magic, Boscastle, Cornwall

Explore a world of artefacts linked to the world of witchcraft and magic in a well-presented Cornish museum

Cornwall. The home of sun, sand, surf and, er, the supernatural. Now, we know holidaymakers bringing their suncream and surfboards to the Southwest are partial to fish and chips and building a sandcastle or two. But how about getting up close to a Ouija board, crystal balls and tarot cards? It may not be traditional seaside fare, but the Museum of Witchcraft and Magic in Boscastle has become one of the best-loved attractions in this wonderful county.

The unusual and spooky museum was opened in the 1950s by Cecil Williamson and has moved location several times. It was to be set up in Stratford-upon-Avon but there was much local opposition, so the collection then went over the sea to the Isle of Man, eventually settling into its current Boscastle home in 1960. Although not everybody was happy with having a witchcraft attraction in the area, the museum has now established itself as one of the best independent museums in the country. It's certainly one of the most unusual, packed with exhibits that are equal parts mysterious, fascinating and chilling. One of the most unusual things to be displayed in the museum was an actual, real witch. The skeleton of Joan Wytte – known locally as the 'Fighting Fairy Woman' at the turn of the 19th century – was a very curious exhibit here until new owners arrived in the 1990s and decided to give her a proper burial.

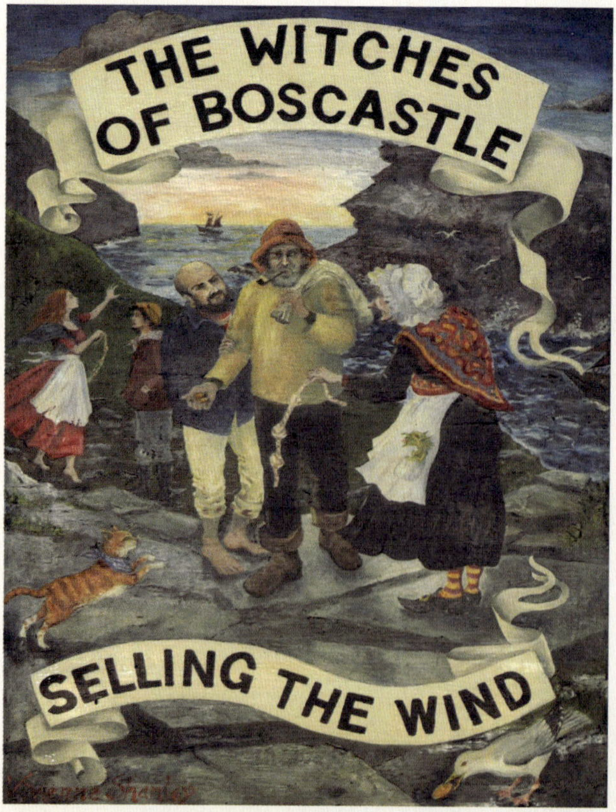

LEFT Heading down, down the Witch's Road to Boscastle.

Taking a look inside the museum today is a must for anyone interested or simply curious about the world of witchcraft, the power of magic or the tools linked to the occult. There are several witch bottles on display – small ceramic or glass containers that were filled with bodily items like hair or nails and buried in a bid to keep away frightening spirits or thwart curses. They were used by many people during the 16th and 17th centuries. You'll also see poppets used by witches. These are often mistaken for voodoo dolls but were instead small figurines used in magic to influence other people, in ways to either heal or harm them. Particularly fascinating are the Books of Shadows, handwritten journals used by modern Wiccans and containing spells and rituals. Moving into darker territory, there's a collection of altar tools that have had a function in rituals for both historical and modern-day witches. Look out for wands, chalices and ceremonial knives. Tarot cards, crystal balls and scrying mirrors should be added to your list of things to see. And while the use of wax figures in small attractions can sometimes be a little too cheesy, this museum does very well as it uses them to show what the home of a 'cunning woman' would have been like.

For those old enough to remember the heartbreaking sight of Boscastle's devastating 2004 flash floods, the museum was at the forefront of the tragedy. Staff were among the first to raise the alarm and witnessed the building suffer severe damage. Despite this heavy blow, an extensive renovation programme was started, and the museum came back even stronger. It's popularity today is testimony to how many people have an interest in witchcraft, both those who are casting a curious eye over the world of curses and hexes as well as those for whom this topic is perhaps a lot more personal. You'll leave with many thoughts and questions about the power of witchcraft and magic in the modern world.

THE HARBOUR, BOSCASTLE, PL35 0HD
WWW.MUSEUMOFWITCHCRAFTANDMAGIC.CO.UK

02 Charlotte Dymond Memorial, Roughtor, Cornwall

Take a walk to Cornwall's second highest peak, where a murder memorial stands and the victim's ghost has been sighted

A windswept Bodmin Moor. Sunday 14 April 1844. A young female servant has been brutally murdered by her boyfriend. The sickening news so outrages the local community that thousands turn out to see the perpetrator hanged at Bodmin Jail. A memorial is put up to remember the tragic end of Charlotte Dymond. But her story doesn't end there. Far from it. Chillingly, it's said that on the anniversary of her death, Charlotte's spirit can be seen walking near the murder scene at Roughtor, dressed in her Sunday best.

Charlotte Dymond worked at Penhale Farm on the edge of Bodmin Moor and had started a relationship with fellow

live-in servant Matthew Weeks. They went for a walk out on the moor during that fateful Sunday, but only Weeks was to return to the farm. A week went by and, during that time, he made up a story about Charlotte going to work in a different house. On the following Sunday, Weeks himself went missing, fuelling speculation that he had killed his girlfriend. When the farmer's wife found his shirt, it seemed beyond doubt – the collar was torn off, buttons were missing and spots of blood were on it. A search party went onto the moor and discovered Charlotte's body at Roughtor, the second highest peak in Cornwall. Her throat had been cut from ear to ear.

The hunt started for Matthew Weeks and he was eventually tracked down in Plymouth, where he was staying with a family member. He was returned to Bodmin to face trial, pleading not guilty. The jury was not convinced, though. They took just 30 minutes to return a guilty verdict and Weeks was sentenced to death by hanging. He was held at Bodmin Jail for ten days before being executed there. Evidence suggests as many as 5,000 people turned out to watch him hanged on 12 August 1844. Hanging was common in those days and they were often popular public events, but this is an especially large number of people to turn out for an execution in this part of the country.

To reflect the public outcry, a memorial was placed on Bodmin Moor close to the murder scene. An inscription explained the terrible events. Weeks was buried in the coal yard at Bodmin Jail, while Charlotte was laid to rest at Davidstowe Church.

We may never know the full details of what went on when this young couple embarked on that fateful walk on the moors, and a young woman was shockingly killed in her prime. This corner of remote Bodmin Moor, however, is still very much alive with her story.

ROUGHTOR CAR PARK, ROUGHTOR ROAD, NEAR CAMELFORD, PL32 9QG, THEN A WALK UP THE HILL

OPPOSITE From ruined buildings to misty moors, Cornwall is one of our spookiest counties.
BELOW The Charlotte Dymond memorial is an eerie reminder of terrible events.

03 Bodmin Jail, Cornwall

Be courageous and explore this famously haunted Cornish jail after dark on a ghost hunt

The location is as spooky as it gets; on the edge of the remote and mysterious Bodmin Moor, an area riddled with dark legends. Few places feel as creepy when the mist starts to roll in. And here, in 1779, during the reign of King George III (r. 1760–1820), a formidable and notorious prison was built from granite. So imposing and intimidating was this structure that it became one of the most feared prisons in the country over the next 150 years. Many inmates sent here had committed minor offences, but this jail also housed plenty of murderers and even some pirates. It was also a holding area for convicts being sent overseas to Australia. Despite being a trailblazing place for incarceration, inmates had to endure terrible conditions, and more than 50 were executed for their crimes within these walls. With such a fascinating and often gruesome past, it's unsurprisingly one of Cornwall's best-loved tourist attractions. But those buying tickets for Bodmin Jail are not just holidaying families wanting a bit of horrible history; this Cornish jail has such a reputation for hauntings that it attracts paranormal enthusiasts from around the world.

Among the spirits you may encounter on a visit to the jail is that of Selina Wedge, executed in 1887 for the murder of her son. The story goes that Selina drowned her child after being persuaded to by a lover, who did not want the

responsibility. Both staff and visitors have reported seeing her ghost wandering the prison and hearing her crying. The hottest spot for the sightings is by the place she spent her last days. You may well be overcome with sadness here. Several have been.

ABOVE The ruins of the jail, where many spent unhappy years.
OPPOSITE Bodmin Jail has the perfect ingredients for a spooky family day out.

It's possible you may also come across the last person to be executed in this jail, a murderer called William Hampton. He killed his girlfriend and was hanged in 1909, but some reckon his restless spirit still haunts the jail. Will you be one of the visitors who report seeing a shadowy figure near the execution area and feel like they are being watched? Be alert all through your tour around Bodmin Jail; it may be that you hear unexplained and frankly unwanted sounds such as whispers and the clinking of chains that can scare folk in a way Jacob Marley never managed. And stay alert for the sudden temperature drops around the prison cells – many of which have spooky tales attached to them. Paranormal investigative teams have recorded some alarming noises and cold spots in the cells.

If you want to go for the less creepy approach, you can visit the jail during daylight hours. But Bodmin Jail has embraced its haunted heritage and organises a number of different ghost tours that introduce visitors to some of the most famous spectres in Cornwall. The 90-minute ghost walk with a paranormal expert will have goosebumps rising on your neck. You'll be constantly checking behind you to see if you're being followed. Under-12s are welcome as long as they're with an adult – preferably one who won't run away. If you're super brave, ask yourself if you can stomach the after-hours ghost tour. This one is 18+ only and lasts four and a half hours. During the tour you'll be with expert ghost hunters and you'll have use of ghost hunting equipment to explore the darkest corners of the jail on your own. You'll get to hear plenty of spooky stories along the way and, as you can imagine, it's not for the faint-hearted. Keep an eye on the website around Halloween for all sorts of special events.

BERRYCOOMBE ROAD, BODMIN, PL31 2NR
WWW.BODMINJAIL.ORG

04 Buckland Abbey, nr Yelverton, Devon

This home in the Devon countryside is said to be teeming with ghosts, including one belonging to seafaring legend Sir Francis Drake

Buckland Abbey has had several uses since it was established in the 13th century, from Cistercian monastery to the home of a famous explorer. It's regarded as one of the most haunted sites in the UK and is open to visitors, if you can stomach the legends surrounding it. Many a chilling ghost story has its origins within the walls of this historic building found in the beautiful rolling countryside of Devon. Its story begins in 1278 when it was founded as a Cistercian monastery by Amica, the Countess of Devon. But its time as a monastery came to an end in the 16th century, during the Dissolution of the Monasteries under King Henry VIII (r. 1509–1547), and it was sold to become a private home, with architects significantly reshaping it. It later became home to the world-famous seafarer and defeater of the Spanish Armada, Sir Francis Drake.

The oldest hauntings date back to the Cistercian era, however. Monks have been spotted walking through walls of the country home – well, they would do, because the original layout had the doors in different places. Much of the paranormal intrigue at Buckland Abbey focuses on the kitchen of the modern house, where one particular cook can't seem to abandon her old life as a servant.

Pots and pans have been known to move, a chair sometimes rocks on its own and doors slam when nobody is about. The ghost in the kitchen is not a threatening one, but some people have been so severely affected by the presence they have been unable to stay there.

The most famous spectre to inhabit Buckland Abbey is that belonging to Sir Francis Drake, and there are enough supernatural stories swirling around Drake's reputation to make this a hotbed of ghostly action. According to legend, Drake made a pact with the devil in exchange for his unrivalled naval skills. The rumours of his dealings with demons and black magic have been passed down through the centuries. Was this the reason he was able to defeat the Spanish Armada so emphatically and rebuild the abbey quickly and efficiently? Probably not, but it is startling how these satanic rumours have existed for so long.

And so to Sir Francis Drake's ghost. It's been spotted numerous times and takes the form of a shadowy figure, often walking the corridors at night. Sightings have also included ghostly dogs and horses, wrapped up in the legend that Drake was in league with dark forces. Some claim there is a pack of phantom dogs that prowl around with Drake's spectre, minions of the devil with red eyes that are set on collecting souls of the damned. Drake's drum is kept in the house and is said to beat in times of national crisis. Other local stories insist Drake is driving a black coach pulled by fiery horses across Dartmoor to

BELOW Sir Francis Drake is said to be one of many ghosts at Buckland Abbey.

Buckland Abbey. In a remote and desolate environment well known for accounts of beastly animals, these links to Sir Francis Drake are in good company.

One of the best places to investigate paranormal activity is in the Great Hall, where at least two ghosts are known to dwell. The first is that of a man called Charles, who was here in the 1800s but sadly fell to his death while up high working on the ceiling. Since this tragic accident, his presence is said to linger around the fireplace and not stray far from it. Another spirit hanging around in the hall belongs to a woman called Catherine, but her demise was no accident. She was drowned in a lake by her husband and her sorrowful figure appears to be trapped within the hall. Buckland Abbey seems to have a right old mix of spooks living within its walls, enough to rival the spectre-filled house in the BBC sitcom *Ghosts!*

YELVERTON, DEVON, PL20 6EY
WWW.NATIONALTRUST.ORG.UK/VISIT/DEVON/BUCKLAND-ABBEY

05 Tyneham Village, Wareham, Dorset

Stroll through an abandoned village, where people left their homes as part of the war effort and never returned to live in them

There was once a thriving community in the village of Tyneham, close to the Dorset coast. A church was busy with worshippers on Sundays, a local school kept children on their toes during the week and communication with the rest of the world took place through the post office and telephone box. Now the population of Tyneham is exactly zero. Nobody lives here. It's a ghost village and perhaps the spookiest settlement you'll find on these shores.

There are few places you can safely visit where a whole community has been ordered to leave, trapping the buildings in time. But Tyneham is one. As well as being unique in its abandoned creepiness, resulting in the creation of a kind of 'lost world', Tyneham is also a testament to how much people were prepared to sacrifice to help defeat Germany in the Second World War. The order came in November 1943. The 225 villagers were put on notice, given 28 days to gather their belongings and relocate. The village – all of its buildings and surroundings – were needed for training exercises as the Allies started to prepare for the pivotal D-Day operation. The last of the villagers was ordered to move out of Tyneham just before Christmas, on 17 December. They thought it was a temporary measure, that they'd be able to return to their homes when the war was over. Wardens at the church even left a note on the door for the soldiers due to train there. It read: 'Please treat the church and houses with care; we have given up our homes where many of us lived for generations to help win

the war, to help keep men free. We shall return one day and thank you for treating the village kindly.' But they never did return to live in these homes.

In 1948, a compulsory purchase order ensured the village would stay in the ownership of the Ministry of Defence, and it is still in use for military purposes today. The village is, however, now open to visitors most weekends and public holidays. Most of the houses have lost their own battle with the elements, now standing as ruins, the local flora and fauna taking over. But the church and the school are still intact and serve as museums, complete with displays about the village history. There are also interpretive boards along The Row explaining who lived in each of the terraced homes on that stretch.

As you might imagine for a village that has experienced so much upheaval, paranormal enthusiasts have recorded several strange occurrences here – from voices and whispers heard near the school to phantom footsteps pattering around the village ruins, from mysterious cold spots to apparitions of former villagers. But Tyneham doesn't need ghosts to be spooky. The history of this abandoned village and an eerie walk around the buildings is enough to raise goosebumps.

ABOVE Coming like a ghost town... Tyneham has a uniquely mysterious feeling.

FOR OPENING TIMES AND DIRECTIONS, VISIT WWW.TYNEHAMOPC.ORG.UK

06 Dorchester Prison, Dorset

Step inside the dark corridors and rooms of this former prison, in which executed criminals are still thought to roam

On a tour of Dorchester Prison, you can easily picture the scene. Hundreds of people gathering around the gallows, waiting for the executioner. He's soon to appear, taking this latest condemned prisoner to the death drop for a very public end. The inmate in question is one Elizabeth Brown, a grocer whose husband had repeatedly whipped her. Brown got her revenge by attacking him with an axe. But there was no mercy for Brown's predicament; she was found guilty of murder and hanged in 1856, a crowd of locals looking on.

Public executions provided a popular day out for blood-thisty folk in the 18th and 19th centuries. Plenty took place here in the grounds of Dorchester Prison. The last person to be hanged here – and indeed the last person to be executed in Dorset – was James Searle, who was found guilty of murder. But the tide was turning on capital punishment. Victorians

BELOW All the spaces in Dorchester Prison fill you with an uneasy sense of history.

no longer wanted the ugly drama of public execution. Author Thomas Hardy was part of the 3,000-strong crowd who watched the death of Elizabeth Brown. He was disturbed by it, writing about a cruelly unjust execution in his 1891 novel *Tess of the d'Urbervilles*.

Hundreds of years before Dorchester Prison was built, a castle stood at this location, between 1154 and 1290. The prison was constructed in 1795, and it remained a working prison until its closure in 2013. Being sent to Dorchester was a blow for any convict – and a deterrent for would-be criminals. Living conditions were difficult here, and this is precisely why it has the reputation of being one of the hottest sites for ghostly activity in the region. Figures have been seen in the dark, swirling mist captured on camera, and there have even been regular interactions with spirits on the other side thanks to paranormal equipment.

In the final years before its closure, the prison was receiving prisoners from courts in Dorchester, Poole and Bournemouth. Half were convicted and the rest came on remand. Conditions had always been tough for the inmates, but the further back you go, the more horrific the tales you will come across. Suffice to say, there are many tortured souls who had a torrid time here – and some of them are refusing to let go. If you dare to delve deeper, you can take a guided ghost tour, where the spooky stories flow thicker than a ferocious mist on the nearby moorland.

NORTH SQUARE, DORCHESTER, DORSET, DT1 1JD
WWW.GLOUCESTER-PRISON.CO.UK

07 Glastonbury Tor, Somerset

Take a walk to the summit of this very special Somerset hill, steeped in myths and mystery, buzzing with spiritual energy

Glastonbury may be the centre of the universe when it comes to live festival music, but it's also a big hitter in the paranormal world of mystery and spiritualism. Few places are associated with so many high-profile myths and legends, with many of them concerning the small hill known as Glastonbury Tor. This site has been a place of worship for centuries, and an entire book could be dedicated to the mystical stories surrounding it, but we have one chapter. So, let's briefly explore why a visit here may make your hair stand on end.

This is a site special to Christians as well as Pagans. In old Celtic beliefs, there was a hidden cave beneath the hill; enter it and you reach the fairy realm of Annwn. In there, should you find it, you'll be in the home of Gwyn ap Nudd, Ruler of the Celtic Otherworld. Among other nicknacks in his home, there is the Cauldron of Rebirth – a magical receptacle that can resurrect the dead. But that's not all. Legend states the Holy Grail is buried here too. That's right, *the*

Holy Grail, the cup from which Jesus drank during the Last Supper. The one that is said to provide eternal life for those supping from it. The one featured in the 1989 hit movie *Indiana Jones and the Last Crusade*. The one hunted by King Arthur and the Knights of the Round Table in 1975's *Monty Python and the Holy Grail*. What on Earth could it be doing here?

Well, the legend was born in the 13th century, when people began speaking of Joseph of Arimathea travelling to the area with a young companion who went by the name Jesus. Yes, *that* Jesus. These stories inspired the poet William Blake to write his epic *Jerusalem*: '*And did those feet in ancient time walk upon England's mountains green? And was the holy lamb of God on England's pleasant pastures seen?*' While the answer to those questions is probably 'no', it gives an insight into why this is considered a spiritual location.

Enter King Arthur and his Knights of the Round Table, who pursued quests for both the Cauldron of Rebirth and the Holy Grail. Why have one when you could have two, right?

Glastonbury Tor has long been associated with the legend of King Arthur, as it's thought to be the location of what in the stories is the Isle of Avalon, where Arthur faced his last battle. At the time of the Round Table, the distinctive hill would have been surrounded by marshland and suffered frequent flooding, rising high above the surrounding land to gain the appearance of an island. In 1191, the

monks of Glastonbury discovered two bodies here that they thought belonged to King Arthur and Lady Guinevere, fuelling the fascinating stories about the tor.

The tor is, of course, synonymous with the tower standing atop it. The two fit together so perfectly, it's hard to imagine one without the other. But the tower was not built in the way we see it now; originally it formed part of a 14th-century church dedicated to St Michael, although now only the tower remains. Before that, another church occupied the site but was destroyed in an earthquake. Going even further back, the hill was used by Romans. So, its appearance may have changed along the way, but the relationship between humans and the land here is longstanding. Get up close to what remains of the old tower and you'll get a glimpse into how it was once ornately decorated. Look for the carving of St Bridget milking a cow. And then gaze around the horizon, take in the peaceful setting, and breathe in the centuries of myths and legends.

CAR PARK ON CHILKWELL STREET, GLASTONBURY, BA6 8DB, IS 0.8KM (0.5 MILE) WALK AWAY
WWW.NATIONALTRUST.ORG.UK/VISIT/SOMERSET/GLASTONBURY-TOR

BELOW With so many legends, is the energy on Glastonbury Tor more than a feeling?

08 Shepton Mallet Prison, Somerset

Only the bravest will dare to take a tour here, the most haunted prison in the world

Sometimes even the promotional literature of a spooky attraction manages to put you on edge. Shepton Mallet Prison markets itself as the most haunted jail in the world. With a 400-year history and a long list of well-established spooks, the building can certainly lay claim to this scary accolade. Many grisly events have taken place in this Somerset penitentiary over the centuries, and many of them are as gruesome as you can imagine. We're talking murder of inmates, painful torture methods, and let's not forget the hangings carried out inside these secure walls. Fortunately, when you step through the gates at Shepton Mallet Prison you won't be led to your cell like the inmates in days gone by. You get a much better deal and are met by an informative tour guide, albeit one with some chilling stories up their sleeve. And now for the bad news: they're going to lead you around this spooky prison by torchlight. That's right; the corridors and cells are darkened for the ghost tour, giving your night a little extra fright. Reckon you're still up for it? Let's first have a look at who you might meet and then see if your will is strong enough…

The most haunted part of the prison is undoubtedly C Wing, and much of the tour focuses on this spooky area. Once the female section of the prison, it is home to one of the best-known spirits to inhabit the building – the 'White Lady'. A heartbroken woman who was convicted of murder and linked to some troubling stories of betrayal, she has been spotted travelling through the corridors where her fellow female convicts were detained. In her wake, you may feel a cold chill and slight wind. This is possibly the reason why staff at the prison recommend you bring warm clothes and

BELOW Doing time: are you brave enough for Shepton Mallet Prison?

somebody else's hand to hold – preferably still attached to a loved one.

Other spirits you may come across include that of a child; cries of a young person have been heard in parts of the prison. And in the execution room, sudden surges of cold air have been felt by people on tours. Does this signify the spirits of those prisoners are present? You may want to book in for an evening of paranormal ghost hunting to find out, joining a team with professional equipment hoping to capture evidence of something from beyond the grave. Some paranormal investigators hope to catch sight of Ronnie Kray's hand. The notorious gangster spent time in Shepton Mallet, and there's speculation that his hand still appears from time to time...

If you really do have nerves of steel, then maybe you have what it takes to sleep over in the world's most haunted prison. After being given your bedding, you'll spend the night behind bars before being woken for roll call at 7am. The prison hasn't been converted into a hotel, so the experience is basic but authentic – while not costing as much either! And who can argue with that? After all, this was a prison designed to be a deterrent, not offer creature comforts. Check the website for details.

ABOVE Shepton Mallet Prison's interior is a moment trapped in time.

FRITHFIELD LANE, SHEPTON MALLET, SOMERSET, BA4 5FQ
WWW.SHEPTONMALLETPRISON.COM

09 Gough's Cave, Cheddar Gorge, Somerset

Step inside this beautiful Somerset cave in a grisly gorge, where cannibal humans once roamed

Deep in the heart of one of the UK's most stunning natural landscapes, the discovery of hugely significant human remains helped archaeologists to piece together a gruesome story of ritualistic cannibalism.

Cheddar Gorge is home to jaw-dropping cliffs, enchanting caves and incredible rock formations, understandably pulling in nature fans from around the world. But, in 1903, a discovery in Gough's Cave gave the Gorge an important place in not only natural geology, but also human history. Crawling through tight spaces and aided only by candlelight, what cave explorers stumbled upon helped us get a glimpse into the lives of our ancestors – and not everything they saw was easy to comprehend.

Fairly close to the entrance of the cave, a skeleton lying on the ground was found to be the oldest ever discovered in the UK. Dated to 10,000 years old, it became known as 'Cheddar Man'. A number of other human bones were also found in the cave – some displaying signs of butchery. Yes, butchery. It meant that here, in beautiful Somerset surrounded by stunning countryside, there was evidence of cannibalistic behaviour.

We now know cannibalism in Gough's Cave dates back nearly 15,000 years. Some of the human bones found here in the 1980s featured cut marks, suggesting that flesh had been removed using primitive tools. What's more, some bones had been cracked open to extract the marrow. Some of the skulls found in the cave had even been modified into cups, which suggests a ritualistic meaning behind the gruesome events.

Cannibalism was not prevalent in Britain (and we don't consider it normal behaviour these days, although drinking from skulls by academics in one Oxford University college has only recently stopped), and yet we have a situation here where one of the people involved was as young as three years old. But, truth be told, we don't exactly know why humans turned on each other to consume their flesh. It could have been a means for survival – the Ice Age had not long ended, food could well have been in short supply and so cannibalism

LEFT Gorge yourself on the creepy caves at Cheddar.

may have been a necessity. Or perhaps the cannibalism was ritualistic, with people honouring their dead by consuming them. Another theory suggests territorial conflicts could have played a part, and that those who were cannibalised may have been captives who were victims of violence. All these theories and more are explored in the Cheddar Gorge Museum of Prehistory, further down the road. Whatever the reason, standing in Gough's Cave and learning about England's cannibalistic history is enough to give you the shivers.

You can buy tickets to head inside Gough's Cave and see for yourself where the historically important bones were found; it's a gorgeous natural feature, but the cave feels extra creepy once you know what went on here…

CHEDDAR GORGE, THE CLIFFS, CHEDDAR, SOMERSET, BS27 3QF
WWW.CHEDDARGORGE.CO.UK

10 The Ancient Ram Inn, Wotton-under-Edge, Gloucestershire

What used to be a historic inn serving up delicious drinks is now a specialist haunt for paranormal investigators serving up spooky shocks

If you build an inn on an ancient pagan burial ground that sits on the ley lines running straight to Glastonbury, then you're probably asking for trouble. I guess planning rules in the 12th century didn't take account of such matters as, over the centuries, the Ancient Ram Inn has become what many consider to be the most haunted pub in Britain. I say 'pub', but technically that's not true; trading ceased here in 1968 and there's no longer a friendly landlord waiting to welcome you with a pint and a roaring fire. The inn has remained abandoned ever since, save for a short period of time when it opened as a guest house. You see, the reputation of this place got the better of the business; only the supernaturally curious would want to venture inside this building now, and even many of those would run a mile at the first sign of action.

However, it is still possible to venture inside. And if you're brave enough, you can even stay the night. But you'll have to do this through a specialist ghost-hunting company, which hires the building for investigations. The chances of the Ram reopening as a pub that serves up Sunday carveries are slim: this place is not for the faint-hearted, nor is it even to be joked about. Proceed with caution – and only if you are in the market for genuine scares.

If you do decide to step inside the old inn as part of a small group of ghost hunters, you're likely to be outnumbered by the spirits that call this building home. There are thought to be upwards of 20 ghosts in this former hostelry, some with an incredibly dark reputation. Every single room here is linked to a supernatural story. Literally nowhere is safe.

Let's start with the Witch's Room, where a woman accused of witchcraft in the 15th century attempted to take refuge from those wanting to execute her. But it was to no avail, for she was dragged out of this room and burned at the stake. Her restless spirit is associated with sudden drops in temperature and visitors have spoken of hands pushing against them.

BELOW The old inn is one of the most haunted buildings in the country.

The Bishop's Room is considered the most haunted; within its walls dwell as many as nine spirits, including that of a former monk. Screams have been heard here, a woman has been seen hanging from the ceiling and a Roman Centurion appears to pass through the walls. Hardened ghost hunters have been scared out of their wits in this room. But there's no hiding anywhere you go in this inn. Run upstairs, and you'll be in the company of a murdered woman's spirit, known for issuing all kinds of terrifying noises.

As a ghost-hunting experience, though, this is in the supernatural equivalent of the Premier League. When you turn up for your late-night tour, expect the investigators to give you an overview of the building's history and key areas of activity. You'll be using a wide range of specialist equipment to tap into the inn's spooky secrets, including that used in electronic voice phenomena (EVP) recording, EMF meters (which detect fluctuations in the electromagnetic field), infrared cameras and thermal imaging. Some tours hold a séance in the Witch's Room, a dark activity that has led to numerous chilling responses. Knowing all this, you'll do well to get through the door in the first place – let alone stay into the night for the duration of the paranormal investigation. It's no wonder the owners struggled to run it as a bed and breakfast.

POTTERS POND, WOTTON-UNDER-EDGE, GLOUCESTERSHIRE, GL12 7HF
WWW.ANCIENTRAMINN.CO.UK

11 Avebury Stone Circle, Marlborough, Wiltshire

This well-preserved henge is so large it has a village inside it – and a whole lot of haunting tales to keep you on your toes

There are stone circles and then there is Avebury Stone Circle. When it comes to sheer scale, Avebury is in a totally different league to sites like Stonehenge. Dating back to at least 2200 BC, this Neolithic behemoth is an unbelievable 330m (1,083ft) in diameter, while there are nearly 100 huge sarsen stones here, some weighing more than 40 tonnes. It's a giant of a stone circle (in fact, it contains three stone circles), and it has some larger-than-life spooky stories to match.

This mystical, awe-inspiring location is different from most other stone circles in that life goes on within it. There are people who literally call this mysterious collection of monoliths their home – there are houses in between them. Many have passed through here over the centuries and, as such, there is much talk of ghostly presences and surges of energy – strange things have been experienced here, so many that I could write an entire book on this spooky site alone. But let's cram in the most we can…

Several visitors to Avebury describe seeing a tall figure wearing dark robes and standing silently by the stones, like some sort of spooky Obi-Wan Kenobi. The fear of dread often comes over those who witness this presence, and he's often thought to be a druid or shaman who used the site many centuries ago. And those stones the druid is standing next to – have they moved since last time you looked? It sounds a bit of a stretch, but plenty have claimed that these massive pieces of rock change place overnight – or in even shorter periods of time. Could this be linked to the enormous levels of spiritual energy said to be found along the St Michael's ley line, which runs through this site?

Of all the sightings reported here, the most common are those linked to the so-called phantom children and their ghostly laughter. Chuckling, giggling, guffawing; it's all been heard, and it's said to emanate from the spirits of children running around the stones. As to the origin of the youngsters, speculation suggests they were the victims of a medieval plague outbreak, or that they were lost or buried in ancient rituals. Either way, according to the reports, they enjoy running around the stones and having fun all these years later.

Perhaps most freaky are the visitors who have wandered around Avebury and

BELOW Avebury Stone Circle actually has a pub within it!

claimed to have entered into a 'time slip'. This is where witnesses find themselves spending a few moments in a different era, seeing the village as it was centuries ago and villagers who are no longer alive. This is one of the strangest experiences reported anywhere in this book.

As well as the stones themselves, the village of Avebury has its own ghostly connections. The Red Lion, a pub dating back to the 17th century and sitting inside the stone circle, is said to be haunted by a woman murdered by her jealous husband in a fit of rage. 'Florrie', a landlady or serving wench, is said to have been thrown down the 26m (86ft) deep well still found inside the pub today (although now covered with a glass top). Grab a seat nearby and peer down into its murderous depths. But before you get comfy and settle down for a pint or two, head to the village church and stand near the trees, where some say you can hear religious chanting and paranormal recordings have been made of spirits calling out names. Perhaps you'll be needing that drink in the Red Lion...

AVEBURY, WILTSHIRE, SN8 1RD

12 **Ghost Walk of the Lanes,** Brighton, East Sussex
13 **St Leonard's Ossuary,** Hythe, Kent
14 **Canterbury Cathedral,** Kent
15 **Dering Woods,** Ashford, Kent
16 **Leeds Castle,** Maidstone, Kent
17 **Hampton Court Palace,** Richmond upon Thames, London
18 **The Clink Prison Museum,** Southwark, London
19 **Crossbones Graveyard & Garden of Remembrance,** Southwark, London
20 **St Dunstan in the East,** City of London
21 **Tower of London,** Tower Hamlets, London
22 **Jack the Ripper Tour,** Whitechapel, London
23 **Theatre Royal Drury Lane,** London
24 **Tyburn Tree,** nr Marble Arch, London
25 **Chamber of Horrors,** Madame Tussauds, London
26 **Highgate Cemetery,** London
27 **The Flask,** Highgate, London
28 **Execution Dock,** Wapping, London
29 **Kelvedon Hatch Secret Nuclear Bunker,** Brentwood, Essex
30 **Epping Forest,** Greater London–Essex border

The East and Southeast

12 Ghost Walk of the Lanes, Brighton, East Sussex

Explore the darker side of this vibrant seaside city on a walking tour of the Lanes

Well known for its seaside charm, independent shops and diverse community, Brighton is perhaps less recognised as being a haunted hotspot. But this busy south coast resort was recently named one of the spookiest cities in the country, so it's well worth plucking up the courage to visit and take part in a ghost walk. When the sun goes down and Brighton's old streets fall quiet, the haunted corners of this seaside city take on a very different feel.

Ghost Walk of the Lanes is a well-established, creepy evening of ghost stories that shouldn't be missed if you enjoy spine-tingling tales about murder, hauntings and unexplained mysteries. They all took place here in the oldest part of Brighton, on a maze of passageways known as the Lanes. The narrow alleys, known locally as twittens, date back many centuries and used to be part of a fishing village. No wonder this area has so many stories to tell.

One of the most notorious stops along the walk is the Druid's Head, one of Brighton's oldest pubs and a place where you can enjoy a pint after the event. But watch out – there have been over 100 accounts of paranormal activity in this watering hole, including that of a poltergeist. Some believe it to be the troubled soul of someone sacrificed by druids. Others say it is the spirit of a smuggler bludgeoned to death in a tunnel leading to the pub. Either way, look out for your friends if you dare to enter.

The Cricketers is another pub with a reputation for things that go bump in the night. It's said to be haunted by the spirit of Robert D'Onston Stephenson, one of the suspects in the infamous Jack the Ripper case. Stephenson lived here in 1888, when it was a drinking den with cheap digs, before going to Whitechapel.

You'll also visit a popular area of common land known as the Old Steine on the tour. Here you can keep an eye out for one of the more horrific apparitions in the city – that of the mutilated mercenary John Robinson, who has been seen lingering in the area. Close by, Steine House was built for George, Prince of Wales to give to his secretly contracted wife, Maria Fitzherbert. The prince had a long-lasting love affair with Brighton and, although the marriage was not officially recognised, Maria lived there until her death and loved the building. So much so, in fact, that some reckon she still lives there and won't vacate her former home – one employee saw an apparition with a powdered wig drift across the lower corridor.

And so to Meeting House Lane for one of the most troublesome tales of the tour. For a sorrowful nun has been spotted here, drifting through a bricked-up doorway, spreading a dark feeling of gloom as she goes. Legend has it she ran off with a soldier and the two young lovers were caught and returned from whence they came. While the soldier was hanged for deserting his post, Sister Agatha had an even more horrendous fate. Like many nuns and monks who transgressed in those days, she's thought to have been walled up and left to die.

Intriguing tales like these will fill your evening in Brighton, with a costumed expert storyteller bringing these stories of death, vengeance and tragedy to life with a dark humour. Special events held here even include a three-course meal in a spooky cellar. Maybe take a friend and hold their hand.

BRIGHTON
WWW.GHOSTWALKBRIGHTON.CO.UK

BELOW Dare you take a guided tour around Brighton's darker sites?

13 St Leonard's Ossuary, Hythe, Kent

Stand before a well-preserved – not to say chilling – collection of human bones

For many people, seeing a human skull is one of the spookiest experiences imaginable. Knowing that what lies before you is not a plastic replica but the remains of a person's real head, you can see why that would creep some people out. Yet there are places around the world that display hundreds of human skeletons and have become a kind of mysterious, dark attraction, pulling in thousands of still-living visitors to peer at the once-living exhibits. The Paris Catacombs are one such eerie example, with skulls packing an underground labyrinth below the streets of the French capital. In Austria, Halstatt Ossuary, or *Beinhaus* (bone house), contains more than 600 once-buried skulls which have since been decorated and put on display. It's so popular, the village has had to take steps to restrict visitor numbers. But don't think displaying human bones is limited only to far-off lands; there are several sites in the UK, but the biggest is hidden away in the Garden of England. That's Kent, in case you were wondering.

St Leonard's Church in the coastal town of Hythe was built at the end of the

11th century and is home to not only the biggest but also the best-preserved skull collection on these shores. Here you'll find the remains of 4,000 people. Although the bones do not form complete skeletons, they are piled very carefully after being rearranged in 1910. Studies reveal most of the bones kept here belonged to women, and around 10 per cent are children. Where they came from is still up for debate, though the likely explanation is that these long-dead folk were living locally in the 13th century when burial space became limited. It's thought the people who had been buried for some time were exhumed, giving up their place in a kind of unconsciously chivalrous, posthumous benevolence. But people do like to speculate about wilder theories of their origin, with some reckoning the bones came from Danish pirates who were killed in a bloody battle. Others suggest they were soldiers who fell during the nearby Battle of Hastings. Another theory goes that these are victims of the Black Death, though this is very unlikely, as those poor people were often placed in quicklime in a bid to stop the spread.

But whatever their origin, the bones of St Leonard's have been a macabre tourist attraction for a long time. This oddly compelling collection was referred to in 17th-century texts, and drawings have been found of the ossuary dating to 1787. In the early 1900s there were postcards that featured some of the bones, indicating how visitors were flocking to experience what was – and still is – an unusual sight. The church charges a fee to see the bones and the display remains as popular as ever. But some people will always try and ruin it for everyone. Such was the case in 2018, when 21 skulls were stolen in a particularly sick and twisted crime. Where the plundered bones ended up, we don't know. They may have been sold on the black market, to illegal collectors who now have a ghoulish addition to their home. Some people, it seems, continue to have an insatiably morbid fascination with death in all its forms.

OAK WALK, HYTHE, KENT, CT21 5DN
WWW.SLHK.ORG/THEOSSUARY

OPPOSITE The bone pile at St Leonard's Ossuary.
RIGHT The skull display at St Leonard's is a jaw-dropping sight.

14 Canterbury Cathedral, Kent

The scene of a murder and home of several ghost sightings, Canterbury Cathedral is at the centre of what many think is a very spooky town

The cathedral dominating Canterbury's skyline is as magnificent as it is massive, an architectural wonder that's a must-see on any thorough tour of the country. For nearly a thousand years this has been one of the most important buildings in the country, and in 1170 it was the scene of a famously brutal murder.

The then Archbishop of Canterbury, Thomas Becket, had excommunicated three bishops, who had broken with tradition to crown Henry the Young King in York. It was a titular reign only, as his father, Henry II (r. 1154–89), refused to grant him autonomous rule. Exactly what the 'new king' said about Thomas Becket is disputed, but there is no doubt as to how it was interpreted by his knights; they took his words as an order to kill the archbishop. As a result, four knights attacked Becket with swords, causing his blood to spill on the floor of the cathedral. A mysterious black mark on a pillar in the cathedral is thought to be the haunting outline of Becket. Accounts say he clung onto it for dear life while being attacked.

Another archbishop, Simon Sudbury, was murdered in London at Tower Hill in 1381 by Wat Tyler, the head of the Peasant's Revolt. Sightings of Sudbury's bearded ghost have been reported in the cathedral tower named after him. The ghost appears pale faced but not headless, which is perhaps surprising given his head was buried in a different place to his body.

There's a passage in the cathedral known as the Dark Entry, and it's here that another ghost is known to hang out – that of Nell Cook. A servant of a canon based at the cathedral, Nell poisoned him and his mistress when she learnt of their affair. As punishment, she was buried alive here under the Dark Entry passage. There have been several sightings of her, with Friday evenings being a particularly active time. Some reckon that those who see her apparition themselves meet with an ill fate soon after, so perhaps

LEFT The haunting outline of Thomas Becket is said to be on one of the pillars.

ABOVE Heart of glass: Canterbury Cathedral's beautiful stained window.
OVERLEAF The cathedral looms large over the city, but it is not the only haunted place in Canterbury.

think twice before seeking out the ghost of Nell Cook.

There are many other haunted spots in Canterbury's old city centre. If you fancy a snack with a side of the supernatural, head to Tiny Tim's Tearoom. This quaint building hides a dark secret: it is reputedly haunted by three children from the Middle Ages. A fire destroyed the building in 1986, and the hauntings came to light during restoration work in the 2000s. Workmen made a grim discovery – the hair and teeth of three children along with the dates they were born and died inscribed in Bibles. The story goes that this reawakened the spirits of the children, and builders began hearing children playing on the staircase and a series of strange sounds coming from the attic. Some said they heard children whispering close to where the hair and teeth were found. It's a chilling tale, made even more spooky by reports of these spectral residents coming into the tea room, moving objects on their own, turning taps on and whispering to the guests. Listen out. You might experience more than just afternoon tea.

THE PRECINCTS, CANTERBURY, KENT, CT1 2EH
WWW.CANTERBURY-CATHEDRAL.ORG

REPAIRS
TIMPSON
Great Service by Great People
Shoe Repairs
Key Cutting
Engraving
Watch Repairs
TIMPSON
Café Mauresque
THE CITY ARMS INN
Aztec
Silver Designs
THE SHAKESPEARE
SHEPHERD NEAME
Lunch Specials

Jack W

15 Dering Woods, Ashford, Kent

A well-used woodland may seem a pleasant place for a stroll, but this one harbours a troubled and dark past that could overshadow your visit

This ancient woodland in Kent is a valuable community asset, popular with dog walkers and those wanting to get away from it all on a refreshing stroll. Dering Wood covers 125ha (310 acres) and is part of a larger complex of woodland and farmland around the parishes of Pluckley, Smarden and Egerton. Marked trails show the routes available for walkers and there are even sections where those with horses can go for a ride. In the middle of the wood, many of these paths cross at a junction known as the King George Star. The Woodland Trust describes it as 'a nature lover's dream'. But for some, this place has been the stuff of nightmares.

Dering Woods are potentially the most haunted woods in the country, so much so that they're also known locally as the 'Screaming Woods', due to the terrifying screams heard coming from the woods at night. For those daring to walk these woodland paths, whispers and footsteps can also be heard, with foggy days seeming to produce the highest number of paranormal tales. The forest is said to be haunted by the souls of those who got

OPPOSITE If you go down to the woods today… maybe take a friend with you.

lost in them and died, among them an 18th-century army officer.

There is also talk of a highwayman's ghost stalking Fright Corner – and he's far from happy. The story tells of locals tracking down and capturing the unnamed highwayman, fastening him to a tree and beheading him. No wonder he's back to torment visitors.

People out walking in the wood have also spoken about mysterious dark shadows darting about them, and strange noises being heard in the distance. In fact, the woods have more than an air of *The Blair Witch Project* about them, and in recent years – thanks largely to online supernatural enthusiasts reposting and speculating about disappearance events in more than one so-called 'creepypasta', where horror legends are created and passed on as if they are real – Dering Wood has attracted a steady flow of paranormal fans and those interested in spooky places. While not always verified, such viral tales and subsequent speculation have led to Dering Wood being seen as a hotbed of supernatural activity.

If the woods weren't eerie enough, all this action takes place close to the village of Pluckley, which was listed in the *Guinness Book of World Records* as having the most ghosts (around 12–14) for a single location, earning it the title of Britain's most haunted village. A must-visit for any fan of spooky goings-on.

USE THE CAR PARK ON SMARDEN BELL ROAD, PLUCKLEY, KENT, TN27 0SY

16 Leeds Castle, Maidstone, Kent

Head inside one of the most beautiful castles in the country and you may see something to make your heart race

Situated between London and Dover, Leeds Castle is an iconic building framed by a gorgeous moat. It's a dream scene for those planning tourist brochures. A fortress has stood here since the 9th century, but it has seen significant changes and development over the years, resulting in this picture-perfect castle. Six medieval queens lived here and it was one of Henry VIII's palaces. It's earned a solid reputation for hauntings, so much so that paranormal enthusiasts love to explore it.

You might imagine an old castle to be haunted by troubled knights or headless warriors, but one of the most oft-sighted spooky phenomena at Leeds Castle is linked to the ghosts of two dogs. Both of them are black retrievers with curly hair, and while one has been known to bring good fortune over the decades the other is notorious for the bad luck that follows it. Both dogs have been spotted regularly by staff, visitors and local residents. Sometimes the visions have been alarming because the dogs seemed to have walked through walls.

Let's take a look at the pooch bringing good luck first of all. The legend goes that somebody was sitting in the window

seat of a bay high up on the castle walls. The phantom dog appeared and began barking furiously, and before long the person rose from their seat to comfort them. At that moment, the bay window collapsed and fell below into the moat. Did the ghostly canine save a life? It seems the rescued person owes it a great deal of thanks.

There's no such life-saving tales when the second dog's spirit appears, with bad luck – or even death – befalling some of those who have seen it. King Henry VI's aunt, Eleanor Cobham, is sometimes blamed for this unpopular animal spirit. She was said to be a witch who used potions and other such witchery, some of which may still hang around the castle and affect the dog all these years later. If you're visiting, listen out for the scampering feet of those two dogs. And hope you get the good one.

Mysterious tales also surround the spiral staircase in the Lower Gloriette. Two experienced castle stewards were working there on a quiet day with no visitors when they both independently heard footsteps running down the stairs. They checked to see if it was a member of the public and they radioed other employees in nearby rooms to find out if anyone had seen them. But there was no trace. The ghostly footsteps remain a mystery.

ABOVE Who let the phantom dogs out? Perhaps you will have a ghostly canine encounter at Leeds Castle.

At the bottom of the main staircase in the castle you'll find the portrait of Charles and Jemima Wykeham Martin (Charles was a Conservative politician who sat in the House of Commons in three periods between 1841 and 1870), and there's a spooky story connected to their daughter, Alice. It is said that Alice had psychic powers and gave superstitious advice to family members in order to keep them safe. For example, she reckoned

that if a hawk was brought into the castle then the owner would soon die. One day, in 1878, a new gamekeeper did indeed bring a hawk into the castle and a few days later, Alice's uncle and owner of the castle had expired.

There have more 'traditional' sightings of ghosts in the castle, too. A female spectre has been spotted gliding along the castle corridor, believed by many to be the Duchess of Gloucester. A female ghost has also been glimpsed in the Queen's Room, this time wearing a long dress and brushing her hair.

Leeds Castle is a fabulously picturesque building with the moat adding to its charm. Enter the castle building, though, and you may need to keep your wits about you. This is a fortress packed to the rafters with ghostly legends. How much has been embellished over time, we may never know. But I wouldn't fancy spending a night here alone. Or even with somebody else, for that matter.

LEEDS CASTLE, MAIDSTONE, KENT, ME17 1PL
WWW.LEEDS-CASTLE.COM

17 Hampton Court Palace, Richmond upon Thames, London

The stunning former home of King Henry VIII has a reputation for housing many royal spectres

Anne Boleyn has to be the most well-travelled ghost in British history. She's been spotted plenty of times wandering around the grounds of the Tower of London (page 56) and has also been known to crop up in other places like Blickley Hall in Norfolk. But the second wife of King Henry VIII (r. 1509–47) spent three years married to the king before being taken off to the tower and beheaded. Much of that time was spent living in the grand setting of Hampton Court Palace, so it's perhaps not surprising that her spirit still lingers in this impressive house. She's been spotted walking the corridors of Hampton Court wearing black and solemnly carrying her head in her hands. Not a sight you'd forget in a hurry.

But, as we know, Henry VIII made something of a habit of getting married and so, perhaps inevitably, there's more than one queen spending eternity floating around this former palace. Jane Seymour managed to deliver what Henry so desperately wanted – an heir to the throne in the shape of Prince Edward in 1537. Sadly, she died a few days after giving birth. On 12 October, Edward's birthday, her ghostly figure may be seen on the Silverstick Staircase, close to where she gave birth.

And then there's the 'Screaming Queen', Catherine Howard. She was accused of adultery and treason. Being Henry's fifth wife, the terrified 19-year-old knew all too well her fate when the guards came to take her away. So she made a run for it, crying out desperately for mercy. The corridor where she ran away screaming is now

BELOW Court in a trap: ghosts from centuries past are still said to roam here.

known as the Haunted Gallery. People have reported hearing her screams, feeling dizzy and even passing out when walking through this part of the house.

There are so many queens to be spotted at Hampton Court Palace, you can almost imagine a spectral version of *Six – The Musical*. Indeed, live performances of the show have taken place on the site, making you wonder if the ghosts were watching the all-singing, all-dancing versions of themselves.

But it's not only queens who stalk these grand halls – a royal servant from the 16th century is also said to haunt the palace. This tragic tale concerns Sybil Penn, Prince Edward's wetnurse. She looked after Henry VIII's daughter, Queen Elizabeth I (r. 1558–1603), when she caught smallpox and had a close run in with death. The queen survived and went on to reign for another 40 years. But Sybil was not so fortunate, also contracting the disease and sadly dying as a result. She was buried in Middlesex, but when her tomb was disturbed during a rebuilding of the church in the 19th century, sightings began at Hampton Court. A tall, hooded figure with her hands outstretched, this was the terrifying sight reported by Princess Frederica of Hannover and one of her guards when she lived there.

ABOVE Many people say they feel somebody is watching them at Hampton Court.

HAMPTON COURT, EAST MOLESEY, SURREY, KT8 9AU
WWW.HRP.ORG.UK/HAMPTON-COURT-PALACE

18 The Clink Prison Museum, Southwark, London

This site of terrifying torture is not for the faint-hearted...

Ever wonder where the saying 'throw them in the clink' comes from? It all stems from right here in central London, on the murky banks of the River Thames. 'The Clink' evolved as the nickname for the notorious prison that was established here in the 12th century and in use right up to 1780. Although we'll never know for certain, it's thought the name came from the sounds the blacksmith made as he hammered shut the chains worn by those incarcerated here. Before long, the name had spread beyond the walls of the jail, and it became common slang for prisons throughout the country. But this troubling yet historically significant building – now a museum – is where the name originated.

To say prisoners were badly treated here is a dramatic understatement. The pain and suffering imposed on those held in the Clink was extreme. As you walk around the museum you'll see some of the gruesome gadgets used to harm criminals, procure confessions and force them to name their accomplices. Though they haven't been used for centuries, just seeing that such cruel torture devices existed at all is enough to send a shiver down your spine. One of the most shocking implements is the 'iron boot'. The prisoner's foot would be placed into it and the surrounding space filled with pieces of wood. Then, water was poured in to swell the wood, causing immense pain usually loss of the foot. Over the centuries, there has been talk of some prisoners inside the Clink taking their own life rather than face their torturer.

ABOVE The torture instruments on display are not for the faint hearted.
BELOW Dare you go through the door at The Clink?

So just what kind of spooky happenings have been reported in the Clink Prison Museum? Paranormal investigators who have spent time here reckon the spirits of many a former tortured prisoner linger here. Visitors have experienced cold spots and overwhelming feelings of dread within its walls. And the noises are worth mentioning, too. The distant screams, whispers and footsteps heard hear are disturbing enough, but the *clink, clink, clink* of chains rattling is surely the most spooky of all spectral sounds. Look out for the 'Lady in White', thought to be the ghost of a female prisoner who was tortured here and died in captivity.

The museum is open during the day, and that's a spooky enough experience. But ghost tours are also available for when darkness falls, the tourists go home, and the Clink falls quiet. During ghost-hunting vigils, visitors have reported doors suddenly closing, glasses smashing and even seeing a woman playing with her chains. Ghost hunters carrying out a table tipping (a practice in which participants sit around a table, hoping for it to be moved, rocked or tilted by spirits) tell of a sock coming out of nowhere and landing on the table. Check out the museum's website for opening times and upcoming events so you that can plan your own spine-tingling visit.

CLINK STREET, LONDON, SE1 9DG
WWW.CLINK.CO.UK

19 Crossbones Graveyard & Garden of Remembrance, Southwark, London

Join the monthly vigil for the 'forgotten dead' of London who were placed in Southwark's mass burial pit

Appalling treatment of society's poorest people happened in death as well as in life during the medieval period. In London, dead paupers and those who were not connected to the church were placed beneath the ground in Crossbones Graveyard – essentially a huge, crowded, unconsecrated burial ground for people of little means or status. It soon became synonymous with those less fortunate in life – the 'forgotten dead'. Among these were the 'Winchester Geese', a name given to the medieval sex workers of Southwark because they were licensed by the Bishop of Winchester, no less. These women worked their trade within the Liberty of the Clink, an area outside the laws of the City of London (as well as what went on in the brothels, other dubious activities took place in the once immoral neighbourhood of Southwark, including the baiting of bulls and bears).

BELOW Pay your respects here to the exploited medieval sex workers.

As many as 15,000 people were buried at Crossbones, and it continued to be used until there was literally no space left. The last body was added in 1853.

Several of London's ghost tours stop here, and there have been occasions when visitors have described sudden drops in temperature, hearing whispers in the night or even seeing the ghost of a young woman in ragged clothes. Could this be one of the Winchester Geese? The people placed in Crossbones at the end of their lives had often suffered considerable injustice and intolerance, and people who are tuned into paranormal events feel a strong sense of energy in the area. This is a fascinating place; as city life continues on all around you, this eerily quiet site is a connection between life and death, between the present and the past.

The fate of the thousands buried at Crossbones, including the Winchester Geese, was brought to public attention when local playwright and poet John Constable wrote a series of pieces about the site in the 1990s. He gave the people confined to this mass burial pit a much-needed voice, and a memorial was built at the entrance on Redcross Way. Today, on the 23rd of each month, a vigil is held for those buried here. The plaque at the memorial may read 'The Outcast Dead', but they are no longer forgotten.

REDCROSS WAY, LONDON, SE1 1TA

20 St Dunstan in the East, City of London

Sit a while and maybe eat lunch in a bombed-out church that now offers eerie solitude in the middle of this bustling capital city

Not all places need scary stories about ghosts and grisly ghouls to be spooky; some already have enough about them to invoke a chill down your spine. This church in St Dunstan's Hill is one such place. Ruined walls now covered with climbing, entwining plants are eerie enough to give you the feeling of being on a movie set – and several directors have indeed chosen this site as a film location. The fact that it's located right in the City of London adds to the mystery and intrigue; workers go about their business, skyscrapers rise up in the background, tourists exit a nearby Premier Inn after enjoying an all-you-can-eat cooked breakfast. Yet while the church is a place of solitude to be enjoyed by people taking a little time out from their busy day, it's also one that has endured tragedy and suffering down the centuries. And so there's a dramatic sense of history to absorb here; these walls have witnessed much.

This former place of worship can be found halfway between London Bridge and the Tower of London and once operated as an Anglican Church. There has been a church on this site since around

OPPOSITE This space offers a quiet place to reflect on the terror experienced here.

1100, with a new aisle added in 1391 and repairs carried out to it in 1631. But disaster struck in 1666 when the Great Fire of London ripped through the city and partially destroyed the church. The famous architect Sir Christopher Wren was invited to participate in the rebuilding project. He added a tower with a Gothic steeple in 1695, and the church was once again open for business. After undergoing a bit more structural work in the 19th century, the real body blow for St Dunstan in the East came courtesy of the Nazis in 1941. London suffered terribly during the Blitz, when German bombers attacked civilian targets as well as strategic ones. Thousands of bombs rained down on the capital and more than 43,000 people were killed, with yet thousands more losing their homes. This church proved to be no sanctuary from the terror of war. It suffered a direct hit, which took out pretty much the entire building, save for the north and south walls, and Wren's tower. It remained an abandoned shell until the late 1960s, when the Anglican Church decided a full rebuild would be too costly. The City of London Corporation took on the building and transformed it into a garden, opening in 1971.

Today the church is a reminder of the struggles this part of the city has endured, but it is also a place that in some way became trapped in time. As well as offering a calm place of sanctuary for all those who visit, the ruined walls and glassless arched-stone window frames have so many stories to tell. While modern life continues apace outside this small urban park, in here the creeping plants slowly take over the ruined church and we are reminded of the delicate balance between humans and nature. The echoes of those who have spent time here down the years are felt by all those who come here today to enjoy this eerie oasis of calm in a once-troubled site, surrounded by one of the busiest urban areas in the world.

ST DUNSTAN'S HILL, LONDON, EC3R 5DD

21 Tower of London, Tower Hamlets, London

Look out for ghostly royalty wandering the grounds of this historic place monument to torture and detention

So much more than just a tower, this formidable and fearful fortress in the City of London has housed a mint, menagerie and armoury over the centuries. But it's best-known for the white keep in the centre of this 4.5ha (11 acres) site, which also gives the place its name. Built by William the Conqueror starting around 1078, one of the White Tower's principal roles was to invoke fear and maintain order among the local population, which it did with aplomb. Many gruesome acts have taken place within its thick stone walls and, unsurprisingly, this is one of the most haunted places in Britain. What's more, these are high-profile ghosts – the celebrity A-list of spectral sightings. Like the Ivy in the afterlife.

Perhaps the most famous of the tower's spooky sightings is that of two frightened young boys, dressed in nightgowns and clutching each other with looks of terror. They've been spotted many times and are thought to be the ghosts of 12-year-old Edward V and his younger brother, Richard. When Edward succeeded to the throne in 1483, the boys went to live in the Tower of London, but Edward's uncle claimed the throne for himself as Richard III (r. 1483–85). The youngsters were taken into the inner parts of the tower and soon disappeared from public life, never to be heard from again. Two skeletons were discovered

BELOW Brothers in arms: the spirits of Edward V and younger brother Richard are said to wander here.

in 1674, and many historians claim these belonged to the two boys. We may never know what actually happened behind the closed doors of the tower, but several sightings of those two ghosts indicate it wasn't pleasant.

Another famous ghost to haunt the Tower of London is that of Anne Boleyn, the second wife of Henry VIII, who was beheaded in 1536. There have been many sightings of Anne's headless ghost wandering through the tower's grounds, including one by a Yeoman warden in the 19th century (Boleyn's ghost gets around the country; it also pops up to say 'boo' at Hampton Court Palace, see page 50).

As well as visual manifestations of ghosts in the tower, screams have been heard to echo around the old walls. Just who these blood-curdling calls belong to cannot be proved, but the terrifying wails of a woman are believed to belong to Margaret Pole, Countess of Salisbury. Her son was a critic of Henry VIII's decision to head the Church of England, and so she was executed. But the end did not go well for her at all. The execution was botched by somebody new to the job. Rather than a swift beheading, the young executioner was forced to hack away with an axe several times over. It is said those screams cannot be unheard.

And if you clock the painful cries of a man on your visit to the tower, are these echoing down the centuries from Guy Fawkes? When his infamous Gunpowder Plot of 1605 was discovered, Fawkes was brought to the tower and brutally tortured to give up the names of those conspiring with him. James I (r. 1603–25, England and Ireland) took a keen interest in the torture and gave permission for it to intensify as the days went on. It's thought that Fawkes ended up on 'the rack', his body very slowly pulled apart, before he was hanged, drawn and quartered. Not surprising that some people can still hear those timeless screams.

TOWER HILL, LONDON, EC3N 4AB
WWW.HRP.ORG.UK/TOWER-OF-LONDON

22 Jack the Ripper Tour, Whitechapel, London

Walk the dark alleys and streets where the notorious serial killer preyed on his victims

It's the autumn of 1888 and darkness has fallen on east London's foggy streets. Mysterious figures move in the shadows as people scurry through Whitechapel. There is an overriding sense of panic in the air; for weeks the newspapers have been full of terrifying stories about women from these parts being butchered in frenzied killings. The perpetrator has been nicknamed 'Jack the Ripper', a name which now strikes fear into the hearts of women walking – and working – these streets. The folk living in those troubled times would surely never have imagined the sick murderer of their nightmares would be world famous some 130 years later, or that we're no nearer to discovering the identity of Britain's most notorious serial killer.

LEFT The Ten Bells pub, where some of the victims drank.

Fans of history and those fascinated by true crime should put a Jack the Ripper walking tour on their itinerary when next visiting the capital (note, several operators offer tours and it's important you read up about them beforehand; some are not for the squeamish and there are often age restrictions in place). As well as telling the story of the most infamous mass murderer in British history, there's a darkly chilling aspect to the evening, knowing the events took place exactly where you're stood. Hearing about the bloody killings from an informative guide and seeing the gory images from the time on a tablet allows you to understand how a moral panic quickly enveloped east London during those dark days. Analyse the clues and see if you can find out who was guilty from the list of suspects identified both at the time and in the decades that followed.

Among the stops on your walk will be Durward Street (formerly Buck's Row), where Polly Nichols was found dead on 31 August 1888. The precision of her injuries sparked fears of a medically trained killer. On Hanbury Street you'll stand close to where number 29 was located – the site of Annie Chapman's gruesome murder that deepened the mystery. In Mitre Square, Catherine Eddowes' body was discovered, a crime which really shocked locals because the police presence had been stepped up by this point. The last victim was Mary Jane Kelly on 9 November, the most brutal of all the murders. You'll learn about this horrific act standing on what was once Miller's Court. Walking down East End alleyways adds to the macabre atmosphere, while you'll also see the Ten Bells pub, which was a regular drinking haunt for some of the victims.

Many who go on the tour have done a lot of research into Jack the Ripper, themselves possessing a detailed knowledge of the victims and suspects. Others come here with just a basic understanding of what happened, ready to learn more. Either way, you're in for an unforgettable, if harrowing, evening. Maybe you can come up with a theory to explain the true identity of Jack the Ripper?

YOU'LL BE GIVEN THE LOCATION FOR THE START OF THE TOUR UPON BOOKING
WWW.JACKRIPPERTOUR.COM

23 Theatre Royal Drury Lane, London

Take a tour around this historic theatre and learn about the hauntings that go on behind the scenes

People have been coming to the theatre on this site to watch performances since 1663 thanks to the Royal Charter from King Charles II (r. 1660–85) that prompted its construction. That first building was smaller than its current counterpart, though. Fires and demolition plans have seen buildings come and go on this patch of prime London theatreland, with the current incarnation of the Theatre Royal opening in 1812. Designed by Benjamin Wyatt, the theatre has since been renovated several times, but the layout remains largely the same today as it was then, over 200 years ago. Shows such as *The Producers*, *42nd Street*, *Carousel* and *Oklahoma!* have all been staged here, delighting audiences from around the world, but not every twist and turn takes place on the stage.

Apart from well-known actors treading the boards, there's a chance you could come across a famous ghost or two while you're inside this much-loved theatre. But just who are the stars of the show that reside on the other side? Well, this theatre's best-known spectre

BELOW Discover what has gone off on the other side of the Theatre Royal's stage curtain.

LEFT Some actors going through this stage door have seen more than they signed up for.

is known as the 'Man in Grey'. Wearing a powdered wig, riding boots, a tricorn hat and the titular grey cloak for which he's known, this ghostly apparition came to be considered a good omen for performers about to take the stage. The productions that have been visited by him tend to have done very well, you see. As for who he is, we can't be sure. There's been talk of a murder victim discovered in the 19th century, but whoever the Man in Grey is, he's known to be responsible for noisy footsteps and a strange mist appearing.

Another friendly ghost is thought to be that of Joseph Grimaldi, a well-known and very popular 19th century clown who performed here and at other theatres. Actors have spoken of feeling a 'guiding hand' if they have stage fright or forget their lines. Could this be the playful Grimaldi ensuring the show goes on in the theatre he so loved?

Things get creepier with talk of the Weeping Woman, and reports of the grim sound of soft crying coming from a dressing room. The troubling noises have also been heard along backstage corridors. Although never seen, this mysterious spirit is known for her mournful sounds and the overwhelming sense of melancholy that surrounds them.

But the most troubled haunting, associated with a shadowy figure and a fatal argument, is that of Charles Macklin's ghost. The 18th-century actor was praised for his role as Shylock in *The Merchant of Venice*, but he is now best known for a row with a fellow actor over a wig in the theatre's green room. Macklin stabbed his colleague through the eye with a cane, killing him instantly. The tragedy overshadowed every role Macklin had ever played – a terrible final act.

So, while seeing a show at the Theatre Royal is always a memorable experience, the *real* show takes place during a backstage tour, when the curtains fall and the theatregoers disperse…

DRURY LANE, LONDON, WC2B 5JF
WWW.LWTHEATRES.CO.UK/THEATRES/THEATRE-ROYAL-DRURY-LANE

24 Tyburn Tree, nr Marble Arch, London

In the centre of the capital, you can stand in the place where thousands were hanged in front of baying crowds

Tyburn Brook – it has all the makings of an idyllic location, doesn't it? Indeed, this was the name given to a small stream that used to run near Hyde Park in London, through a little village also known as Tyburn – or 'place with the elms'. Sounds like it was a great place to go for a picnic, right? Well, perhaps not. What we're looking at here is one of the grimmest historical sites in a capital city rife with dark and gory chapters. Make no mistake, the 'tree' of Tyburn Tree bore no fruit, leaves or blossom. Instead, it referred to a wooden gallows structure where mass hangings took place in front of huge crowds. With thousands watching, up to 24 people could be hanged at any one time on the triangular gallows, designed to turn executions into a conveyor belt of streamlined efficiency. For six centuries, this spot was the most notorious place for public hangings in London; between 1196 and 1783 it's thought somewhere between 50,000 and 60,000 lives were ended on the various incarnations of Tyburn Tree.

Today, Tyburn Tree is located where Edgware Road meets Bayswater Road, although there is no huge memorial to the victims – instead, a simple plaque on the ground is the only reminder of the souls who perished here. Buses go by, workers on their lunchbreaks head to Hyde Park, millions of tourists shop on nearby Oxford Street – most of them oblivious to the historic marker on the traffic island as they cross the road. But although the crowds still gather here, the scene was once a very different one. In order to create a deterrent, the executions that took place at Tyburn Tree were public affairs. Locals were actively encouraged to attend, and it wasn't unusual for tens of thousands to gather in front of the gallows. A seated area is even thought to have been built so the more well-to-do could watch the executions in comfort. In those days, ridding London of its 'criminal underclass' was very much a spectator sport.

Those to be hanged at Tyburn Tree tended to start their last day on Earth at Newgate Prison. If the prison were still in operation, it would take 18 minutes

BELOW Public executions were a popular pastime at this haunting spot.

or so to reach the old execution site by public transport. In the 18th century, however, prisoners would be put on a horse-drawn cart and paraded through the streets on a humiliating journey that could last three hours, thanks to the jeering crowds lining the route. Once at Tyburn, they would catch their first sight of the gallows. Although it's unclear what they looked like when they were first introduced, records show a large, triangular-shaped permanent structure was built in 1571, with the intention of performing executions more efficiently. Up to two dozen people could be hanged at a time, for crimes ranging from murder to stealing cattle. Permanent gallows were used until 1759, then replaced by a version that could be quickly assembled and taken down. The last execution on this site took place in 1783, when robber John Austin met his end here. After that, public executions were moved to Newgate Prison.

Standing on this spot today, it's hard to imagine the horrific scenes that regularly took place here. The bustling streets hide ghastly secrets, but it's that contrast which adds to its modern-day impact. For me, this makes it one of the saddest, most unnerving places in London.

MARBLE ARCH, LONDON W1H 7EJ

25 Chamber of Horrors, Madame Tussauds, London

Come face to face with some of the most infamous villains in history

A visit to world-famous Madame Tussauds is a must-do activity for many enjoying a short break in London. Whether it's Ed Sheeran, Lady Gaga or the current president of the United States, it's fun having a selfie with the incredibly lifelike waxwork figures. But while it's all smiles, camera flashes and laughter in the upper levels of Madame Tussauds, there's a much darker attraction down below that has been taking the breath away from visitors for well over a century.

The Chamber of Horrors is not for everyone. Many children will find the content too disturbing, and some adults will also be seen giving it a wide berth, and a visit is optional (you'll be given the option to enter the more controversial displays or conclude your visit terror-free). But you're going to go in, aren't you? That's why you're here!

Funnily enough, the origin story of the famous waxwork displays is rather macabre in itself. The museum's founder, wax sculptor Marie Tussaud, started out working on death masks of notable figures sent to the guillotine – including King Louis XVI and Queen Marie Antoinette. Horrific in nature and yet incredibly detailed, these masks paved the way for what would eventually become the Chamber of Horrors, which first opened in 1802. Evolving over the decades, it became a stand-alone feature and famous in its own right. It's not

OPPOSITE The horror: this part of the waxworks is only for the brave.

without its critics, however; some say the Chamber of Horrors glorifies criminals by giving them a place in the same waxwork museum where models of sporting heroes, entertainers and even royalty can be found. Certainly some visitors may experience an uneasy feeling as they tour the chamber, and while learning about the history of these crimes is compelling, there's also a nagging doubt about whether it's OK to do this.

As you're in London, the criminals on display have a special, dark relevance to visitors from the UK. You'll find wax models of the Kray twins in an exhibition that evokes the brutality of the capital's mid-century crime scene, while murderer Dr Crippen is also on display. Hanged in 1910 for killing his American wife, Crippen hid her torso inside his London house and tried to leg it to Canada with his mistress. Despite being in disguise, he was arrested when his boat arrived in North America. And, of course, you'll learn about Jack the Ripper, the serial killer responsible for murdering at least five women around Whitechapel in 1888. Never caught or formally identified, Jack the Ripper in the Chamber of Horrors takes the form of a Polish barber who came to England in the 1880s and was a key suspect.

Perhaps most sinister are the genuine artefacts on display in the Chamber of Horrors that are linked to some of the most despicable crimes. You'll see the suit of John Haigh, once worn by the 'acid bath murderer' and bequeathed – by him – to Madame Tussauds. Dr Crippen's glasses are also on display, as is serial killer Dennis Nielsen's TV. Most shocking is the pram used by Mary Eleanor Pearcey to transport her two victims. In 1890, she killed the wife and child of her lover, Frank Hogg, and moved their bodies to Hampstead. Creepily, after the pram was returned to Frank Hogg by police, Marie Tussaud approached him and bought it for £25. Most things in here are disturbing in some way, but it's morbidly gripping nonetheless.

MARYLEBONE ROAD, LONDON, NW1 5LR
WWW.MADAMETUSSAUDS.COM

26 Highgate Cemetery, London

Take a tour around this famous cemetery, the creepy location of horror films and a bizarre real-life vampire hunt

Stepping through the iron gates of Highgate Cemetery in north London will see you embark on a journey into the Victorian fascination with both death and Gothic structures. Highgate opened in 1839 as one of London's 'Magnificent Seven', large cemeteries that were built to combat overcrowded churchyards and provide park-like final resting places in the capital. And, although you're in a busy city, there is an air of quiet calm here, of a place much loved but also sort of abandoned;

the emerald moss and creeping ivy add so much to the scene, it's no wonder film directors love filming here.

Highgate was a favourite of London's 19th-century elite. Scientist Michael Faraday is buried here, as is author George Eliot and the philosopher Karl Marx. The cemetery houses magnificent, ornate tombs and, alongside weathered statues and crumbling mausoleums, they help to create an eerie atmosphere that will stay with you long after your visit. The place became overgrown and unappreciated in the post-war years, but interest in this fascinating urban location was rekindled in the early 1970s when it became the setting for several Gothic horror movies, including *Taste the Blood of Dracula*, *Tales from the Crypt* and *From Beyond the Grave*.

Stranger than any film I've watched, however, was the bizarre case of the Highgate Vampire, which caused a media frenzy, resulting, on 13 March 1970, in a mob storming the cemetery. It all kicked off when two high-profile paranormal enthusiasts made claim after claim in the media about vampires and the undead and, thanks to a few eager journalists,

ABOVE Highgate Cemetery was one of the Victorian Magnificent Seven built in the capital.

cooked up a moral panic. When David Farrant claimed to have seen a spectre in the cemetery and Sean Manchester labelled the imposter a vampire in 1970, it wasn't long before the 'being' became known throughout the land as the 'King of the Vampires'. It was certainly popular with some editors on Fleet Street. When Manchester announced he was holding an exorcism at the cemetery and the news was broadcast on TV, a mob of vampire hunters arrived at Highgate and climbed the walls. Gruesome goings-on continued to occur later in the year when tombs were opened and bodies mutilated in horrific crimes. Thanks to the bizarre media frenzy and onslaught of ghoulish amateur vampire hunters, the story of the Highgate Vampire lived on in several works of fiction. It even popped up as a character in the *Buffy the Vampire Slayer* comic book series, when we learnt it had been in a fight with Buffy's Watcher Giles in 1972.

A walk through Highgate Cemetery today is usually more atmospheric than action-packed, and there is an incredible amount of macabre history within these walls. Many will recognise the Circle of Lebanon from the 2018 fantasy-adventure *Fantastic Beasts: the Crimes of Grindelwald*, part of the Harry Potter universe. Since there's so much to see, make sure you allow enough time to explore both sides of the cemetery and aim to use the guided tour service; the expert knowledge you'll receive from your guide is well worth it.

SWAIN'S LANE, LONDON, N6 6PJ
WWW.HIGHGATECEMETERY.ORG

BELOW Some grave films have been shot here over the years.

27 The Flask, Highgate, London

Order a pint at this notoriously haunted pub and you might get a spirit chaser, too

If you come across a centuries-old pub, you can be sure it has some sort of haunted history or hair-raising happenings. The Flask in London's Highgate has been hosting customers since 1663 and has amassed more than its fair share of spooks over the years. Stories, myths and legends ooze from its walls, as can only be expected in a place thought to have served up drinks to highwayman Dick Turpin, and which counts literary giants Byron, Shelly and Keats as former regulars.

The Flask is one of London's best-known and most iconic pubs. A short distance from the famous Highgate Cemetery, it's developed a fine reputation as a meeting place, where locals and travellers can get hold of good beer and food. But that's not the only reason for its cult status, for this is well and truly a supernatural watering hole.

When it opened as a coaching inn, the Flask attracted weary travellers making their way around the country, as well as locals (it's thought the name came from the small glass bottles used to carry water from nearby springs in Highgate and Hampstead). Over the years, it reputedly became a favourite place for intellectuals to hang out, including philosopher Karl Marx, satirist William Hogarth and poet Samuel Taylor Coleridge. They may have enjoyed discussing the sociopolitical issues of the day over a few glasses of rum or whisky – but they weren't the only spirits to be found in this inn.

ABOVE There are plenty of spirits to encounter at The Flask.

The most famous of the ghosts to have been spotted is that of a Spanish barmaid, said to have taken her own life in the cellar after a romance ended badly. Some claim to have seen the tragic woman, a melancholy figure in period dress, lingering around the stairs to the cellar. Staff down the decades have reported feeling cold spots and hearing sobbing in various locations. And then there's the feeling of being watched, as if she is waiting close by to collect your glass as soon as you empty it.

As if that isn't scary enough, any thick-skinned ghost hunter stepping inside for a brave beer should look out for a Cavalier (we're talking a soldier from the English Civil War rather than the spectre of an old Vauxhall car). He's been spotted several times in the main bar area: tall, with boots and a wide-brimmed hat. Paranormal experts reckon he appears and disappears without warning, but often rattles glasses and causes lights to flicker in his wake. Spooky stuff.

One theory as to why the paranormal activity here is off the charts is because the pub's committee room was at one time used to conduct autopsies. You read that right: medical professionals would come here and cut open recently deceased bodies in order to learn more about them. This wasn't legal, of course, but happened because there was a shortage of corpses for doctors to work on. These doctors and many more benefited from a growth in the lucrative business of body snatching from Highgate Cemetery – yet another grisly part of this pub's history to bear in mind when you pop in for a drink.

With its low ceilings, wooden beams, and plenty of nooks and crannies to hide in, the Flask is brimming with historical charm, which somehow manages to make a ghostly encounter feel much more likely. So, if you like ghosts with your Guinness, boogiemen with your beer and jumps with your Jack Daniels, this is the place for you. Keep away from the cellar area, though. Just in case.

HIGHGATE WEST HILL, HIGHGATE, LONDON, N6 6BU
WWW.THEFLASKHIGHGATE.COM

28 Execution Dock, Wapping, London

This part of the Thames is famously haunted by pirates who met their end on the riverside gallows

London was once the busiest port in the world, an accolade which brought wealth and prosperity to the capital. Of course, opportunity makes the thief, and the city attracted some of the most notorious criminals in the land, who engaged in treacherous behaviour all over town, including along its famous river.

Ships entering the River Thames were running the gauntlet, with pirates in operation along the shores. In 1536, King Henry VIII (r. 1509–1547) ushered in the Offences at Sea Act to deter such dastardly behaviour, meaning anybody found guilty could be hanged at Wapping's purpose-built Execution Dock.

These public executions became a popular form of entertainment. (Grim, isn't it? But this was *long* before Netflix...) Londoners would turn out in their thousands to see petulant pirates paraded to the gallows after being found guilty at nearby Admiralty Court. The hangings were symbolically carried out over the river, and they were brutal. A shorter rope was reserved for pirates, as that meant their necks wouldn't break in the drop – making for a much more gruesome death. The victims' limbs could be seen to 'dance' in the struggle against slow asphyxiation, which became known as 'The Marshal's Dance', named after the High Court Marshal presiding over the execution. Once dead, the victims' bodies were left in the noose until three high tides had covered their heads ... you know, just to make sure the job was done. The most well-known seafarer to be hanged here was Captain Kidd, who was sentenced in 1701 for the crimes of piracy and murder. But his execution did not go according to plan – the rope broke, and he had to wait for a replacement before they could try again. His body was hung and displayed in a gibbet (cage) for many years at Tilbury Docks.

With such gruesome goings-on, there is much talk of ghosts stalking the area where the lives of so many pirates were brought to a grisly end. One of the most common sightings involves a notorious one-eyed pirate captain still defiantly roaming Execution Dock in a tattered tricorn hat and long, well-worn coat. Sightings have occurred on moonlit evenings, the unfulfilled captain gazing out to the water and perhaps thinking that it all could have gone so differently. The eerie sound of clanking chains that once bound pirates has also been heard in the neighbourhood. Echoing off the old walls of these East End buildings, it makes for a mournful tune lamenting the downfall of many a pirate. And when these spirits of the high seas are close, people speak of feeling an intense surge of energy in the air and tingling in their fingertips.

The precise location of London's Execution Dock is disputed, but one of the contenders for this grim site of harrowing death is close to the Prospect of Whitby pub. Head there for a seaworthy rum or two and you'll be able to look out onto the banks of the Thames, where replica gallows stand, a reminder of more lawless days, when bystanders roared with delight to see these sinners of the sea brought to justice.

BREWHOUSE LANE,
LONDON, E1W 2NS

BELOW Many pirates found themselves hanging at the end of a rope by the Thames.

29 Kelvedon Hatch Secret Nuclear Bunker, Brentwood, Essex

Go beyond the blast doors of this Cold War nuclear bunker and you may well encounter shadowy spirits and mysterious noises

At the height of the Cold War, when people were being scared out of their wits by the threat of nuclear conflict, a contingency plan was devised to evacuate the British government to an underground bunker in Essex. Built under extremely high levels of secrecy, not even the local population knew what was going on here; delivery drivers allowed on the site had to sign the Official Secrets Act and from above it was designed to look like a modest detached house was being built on farmland.

This was no ordinary house, though. Go through the door, and you weren't greeted by a hat stand and a portrait of the family. Instead, a large corridor slopes down beneath the ground towards a set of thick metal blast doors. Beyond this lay an alternative future, which thankfully the world never embarked upon. If nuclear missiles had been fired, the government of the day would have been rushed to this three-storey subterranean shelter in the hope it could retain some sort of authority over the dystopian narrative unfolding above them.

Inside is a secret world of operation rooms, dormitories, kitchens and toilets covering three underground floors. There's even a BBC broadcasting office, which would have allowed for emergency updates to be broadcast on Radio 4. The tour around this creepy facility is self-guided, which adds to its eerie nature. You can be walking into rooms designed to be used during a global catastrophe and not a soul

LEFT Stairway to Armageddon in a bunker thankfully never used.

will be around. My experience here was both spooky and goosebumpy. Reading about what to do during a nuclear attack in such a disturbing setting is not for everyone. And yet some visitors here had a much scarier time than that.

Kelvedon Hatch has been the centre of paranormal activity for some time, and ghost hunt companies, including Haunted Happenings (www.hauntedhappenings.co.uk), host evenings here for paranormal enthusiasts hoping to seek proof of contact with the other side. Experts have taken some very interesting EVP recordings at the bunker; so convincing are these findings that some who work here feel uncomfortable walking down the service tunnel on their own. Why? Because shadowy figures have been spotted moving towards them.

Deep inside the bunker, more than 36m (120ft) below the surface, the dorms and medical centre have played host to their own ghostly apparitions. Haunting noises have been heard and poltergeist activity reported. Visiting during the day and seeing this creepy Cold War relic is disturbing enough, but going in darkness and actively looking for the paranormal activity is something else entirely. The nuclear bunker was designed and built to be used during unimaginably dark, scary times. Now, in its modern incarnation as a tourist attraction, it's home to a different kind of horror.

KELVEDON HALL LANE, BRENTWOOD, ESSEX, CM14 5TL
WWW.SECRETNUCLEARBUNKER.COM

30 Epping Forest, Greater London-Essex border

This forest on the London-Essex border is a popular base for recreation – for both the living and the dead...

If you go down to the woods today, you should probably take a few friends with you if you're a nervous kind of person. Epping Forest is the largest wooded area in London, covering approximately 2,400ha (5,900 acres), but it shields a few secrets. While most visitors are unaware of the forest's grisly past (or, at least, not put off by it), those spending a lot of time winding between the trees and along mile upon mile of footpaths and cycle trails know there is something else going on in this place known as the 'Cockney Paradise'.

ABOVE Epping Forest has more going on than you might imagine.

Plan a day walking or biking here, and you too can get to grips with several legends that trouble the reputation of this forest.

The most famous of the Epping Forest ghost stories is linked to Dick Turpin, the well-known highwayman who, despite committing some sickening crimes, has managed to develop a reputation over the centuries as a lovable scoundrel. Although not a Robin Hood figure, he was a charming rogue nonetheless, and said to have had a hideout in the forest, though the precise location of his cave is uncertain (it may have been at High Beech or Loughton Camp). Many passing through the area feared for their safety

ABOVE All shuck up: there is a fiery-eyed dog said to roam the forest.

knowing Turpin was on the loose, but it wasn't just those in horse-drawn carriages that had to be careful. Turpin robbed many homes in the area and became such a problem that people built 'Turpin Traps'. These were doors at the top of the stairs that could be bolted, allowing people to sleep safely in their beds without fear of robbery. One road – Traps Hill – was named for this reason, and it's here that Turpin's ghost is often spotted. He's said to thunder down the road on his horse, Black Bess, dragging a woman behind him. Nice chap. He was

killed in York, of course, so why he haunts this neck of the woods is unknown. Maybe he felt he'd get posthumous rich pickings here.

The solemnly named Hangman's Hill sits at a triangle junction at Avey Lane and Pynest Green. Supposedly, if drivers stop their car at the bottom of the hill and put it into neutral, then the rope of the hangman will pull their vehicle up the hill to the top. This is down to the optical illusion caused by the surrounding landscape – it looks uphill but it actually isn't. It can be a fairly busy road, so those doing it tend to upset the locals as well as the forest spirits.

There have also been several sightings of Black Shuck in Epping Forest, a ghostly dog with fiery eyes. Some say it's an omen of bad luck. Those who spend time around High Beech seem to experience the animal's presence most often.

When you visit the area, you'll probably find yourself on Epping New Road, one of the most haunted stretches in the country. Take care when you're driving along here. Among the sightings have been a headless biker, a horseless carriage and many black shadows. It might be best to navigate this part of the wood during daylight hours.

VISITOR CENTRE ON RANGERS ROAD, HIGH BEACH, LOUGHTON, IG10 4AE

31 **Pitt Rivers Museum,** Oxford
32 **Oxford Castle and Prison,** Oxford
33 **Broad Street,** Oxford
34 **Gloucester Prison,** Gloucestershire
35 **Royal Shakespeare Theatre Ghost Tour,** Stratford-upon-Avon, Warwickshire
36 **Warwick Castle,** Warwickshire
37 **The Bone Crypt at Holy Trinity Church,** Rothwell, Northamptonshire
38 **The Coffin Works,** Birmingham
39 **Dudley Castle,** West Midlands
40 **Cannock Chase,** Staffordshire
41 **Grave of the Last Sin-Eater, St Mary's Church,** Ratlinghope, Shropshire
42 **Shrewsbury Prison,** Shropshire
43 **Hack Green Secret Nuclear Bunker,** Cheshire
44 **National Justice Museum,** Nottingham
45 **Ye Olde Trip to Jerusalem,** Nottingham
46 **The Workhouse,** Southwell, Nottinghamshire
47 **Lincoln Castle,** Lincolnshire

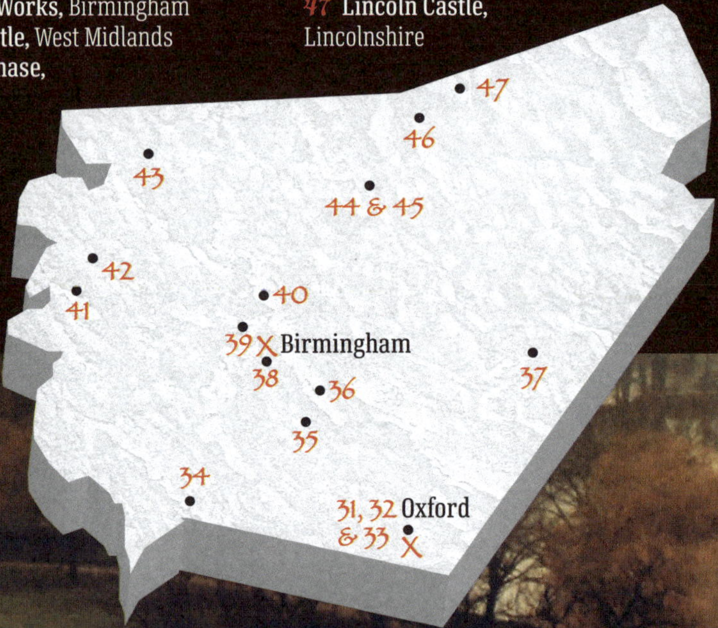

The Midlands

31 Pitt Rivers Museum, Oxford

Get up close to a host of haunted masks and witchy paraphernalia

Amid the cobbled streets of Oxford is a most curious collection. To find it, you first have to enter the city's Natural History Museum, an incredible glass-roofed building housing everything from giant crabs to meteorites. There's nothing too spooky here, apart from the intimidating skull of a *T. rex* and the story of the 'Oxford Dodo', which reminds us how quickly humans can obliterate an entire species. But to see the really creepy exhibits that will stay with you for a lifetime, head to the back corner and go through the mysterious arched doorway that leads to the Pitt Rivers Museum. This is no mere side room at the far reaches of the Natural History Museum. Oh no, this is a full-on museum within a museum, with thousands of exhibits on human life that are as fascinating and sometimes as shadowy as any you'll ever see. Once through the door, the labyrinth of passageways and glass cabinets stretches out before you, as though you've entered a jaw-dropping scene in an *Indiana Jones* film.

This incredible museum was founded in 1884 when Augustus Pitt Rivers gave his collection to the University of Oxford on the condition it be housed in a suitable building and a lecturer employed to teach about it. Pitt Rivers was born Augustus Fox in Yorkshire and served in the Grenadier Guards, but his life transformed almost overnight when he inherited the Pitt Rivers name and a country estate from his great uncle. Now a wealthy landowner, he dedicated himself to collecting obscure objects on foreign trips and buying

BELOW The museum stands out in a city full of beautiful buildings.

RIGHT The Pitt Rivers museum.

interesting items from dealers and auction houses. The result is this cornucopia of weird and wonderful exhibits from around the world.

The first display to make your hair stand on end is the wall of Japanese masks used in Noh plays. Performed exclusively by men and usually with just one actor, Noh theatre combines music with slow, dance-like movement. The masks in the museum date from the 18th century and depict men, women, ghosts and demons.

A little further along you'll see several relatively naturalistic portrait masks of Haida Nation (an Indigenous people of the Pacific Northwest Coast, with traditional territory on the islands of Haida Gwaii, Canada and parts of Alaska) origin. One mask in particular stood out, staying in my thoughts for the rest of the day: it had seemingly gazed at me with its glass eyes, amid an animal-skin beard and long human hair dropping down over its wooden face.

You'll also find exhibits linked to the world of witchcraft and magic. There's a doll commonly found in southern Italy, which is often burnt in the spring to bring luck for the coming harvest; a headdress worn by a priest of Shango, the Thunder God, in Nigeria; a witchdoctor's staff; written charms on both lead tablets and paper, calling upon divine entities to protect the bearer; items used to cast a curse on an unsuspecting victim. And look out for a silver-coloured bottle said to contain an actual witch. While many witch bottles were intended to protect folk from evil, this one belonged to an old woman from Hove, acquired from her in 1915. She reckoned it had a witch inside it and releasing her into the open would cause a heap of trouble. While this seems a tall story, I for one think we should keep the top on and not risk it.

Several years ago, an even more macabre exhibit became the museum's top attraction. The 'shrunken heads', or *tsantsa* – collected from Ecuador in South America – were made when one tribe removed their enemies' skin and hair in order to benefit from their souls and have a bumper harvest. In 2020, museum staff removed them, having decided that exhibiting human remains was too gruesome, and did little to increase the understanding of the Shuar people who created them. A panel explains the decision, but even without the tiny human heads, the Pitt Rivers Museum is still loaded with creepy curiosities for those thirsty for knowledge about our ancestors' strange customs.

SOUTH PARKS ROAD, OXFORD, OX1 3PP
WWW.PRM.OX.AC.UK

32 Oxford Castle and Prison, Oxford

Take a spooky tour around an iconic building known for having more than its fair share of hauntings

The beautiful city of Oxford is globally renowned for its academic excellence and long list of famous university alumni, but it has also endured its fair share of ne'er-do-wells. Those committing crimes in the city – both serious and petty – tended to end up here, in the formidable building that housed Oxford's Castle and Prison. Part of the prison building has now been lovingly converted into the luxury Malmaison Hotel, where you can stay for a comfortable night in one of the original cells, albeit paying a lot more than the original inmates, who got their accommodation for free. A guided tour explores the site, and you'll get a good idea of why this was once a place you'd do anything to steer clear of. Guides tell of characters from the past who are still said to plague this iconic Oxford building in the afterlife. It's a spooky, abandoned place to begin with, but discovering more about its paranormal reputation will send shivers down your spine.

Originally the site of a motte-and-

ABOVE Take a tour of the castle and get creeped out.
OPPPOSITE Oxford's Castle and Prison has many stories in its walls.

bailey castle, this place went on to serve as the county gaol until 1996. The tour of the now-abandoned prison is a fascinating insight into crime and punishment in days gone by, but what really gets the heart racing are the spooky stories. Perhaps the scariest tale of terror is that of an 18th-century woman convicted of poisoning her father. Mary Blandy's story captivated Georgian England, and although she claimed innocence, she was hanged outside this very castle in 1752. As she perished on the gallows, local legend has it that a blackbird sat beside her and sang a song no blackbird has sung since on this spot. Did you hear a blackbird sing a spooky song outside the prison as you ventured inside? I thought not. Now you know why.

And so to the story of George Napier. He was executed for treason in 1620 and was hanged, drawn and quartered on this site, and had his head placed on a spike for good measure. His family recovered his body – aside from his head. Now it's rumoured that Napier's faceless spirit roams the city in search of the missing part, while paranormal investigators are said to have run into his spirit several times.

But much of the ghost-hunters' activity focuses on the site's crypt, where investigations have yielded genuinely unexpected results. Corpses were stored here in the Middle Ages, and a ghostly monk is said to prowl around this part of the site.

If you're not spooked out by the crypt, prepare yourself for St George's Tower, where many ghosts are said to linger. Conditions here during the English Civil War were so bad that overcrowding resulted in hundreds of deaths – and some of the spirits have not moved on.

On the tour, there'll be tales of crime, punishment, escapes and thousands of local folk cheering on executioners who, it's said, were often drunk. Maybe one had to be, to take on such a gruesome job. This terrifying take on history, right in the centre of one of our most beautiful cities, is not for the timid...

OXFORD CASTLE, OXFORD, OX1 1AY
WWW.OXFORDCASTLEANDPRISON.CO.UK

33 Broad Street, Oxford

Stand on the site where Protestant martyrs were burned at the stake

'X' marks the spot on Oxford's historic Broad Street – not of hidden treasure, in this instance, but of macabre executions and centuries of ghostly happenings. The simple brick cross on the ground indicates the site where, in the 16th century, three Oxford martyrs were burnt at the stake after being found guilty of heresy. It happened under the reign of Queen Mary I (r. 1553–58), who was trying to restore England to Catholicism after her father, Henry VIII, had broken away from the Catholic Church. And so, on 16 October 1555, former Catholic priest turned Protestant preacher Hugh Latimer was put to death, flames licking around his body. Nicholas Riddley also met the same fiery end alongside him. He was Bishop of London, and a staunch advocate of Protestantism. Five months later, Thomas Cranmer, who was Henry VIII's Archbishop of Canterbury, was burned at the stake here too. Around the corner at St Giles, the Martyr's Memorial provides a focus for the disturbing events, with statues of all three men taking pride of place in this prominent reminder of their fate. The place where the burnings took place is outside Balliol College; the flames were said to be so ferocious they damaged one of the doors to this, the oldest college in the city. Those scarred, original doors are now within the college, close to the library.

Visitors report the sad cries of the burning martyrs, and shadowy figures appearing close to the cross, especially on the anniversary of the executions. Perhaps most disturbingly, some have experienced the sudden smell of fire and burning

LEFT This 'X' was on fire when the martyrs were killed.

flesh, though it's best to check this isn't coming from the artisan food market that pops up now and again on Broad Street.

Given Oxford's rich history, you should allow time to explore other haunted sites in this esteemed city of learning. Christ Church College (www.chch.ox.ac.uk) was founded by Cardinal Wolsey and is said to house the ghost of King Charles I (r. 1625–1649), who roams the grounds. The king used Oxford as his headquarters during the English Civi War, so you may come across him on a tour of the college. Or head over to the Bodleian Library (https://visit.bodleian.ox.ac.uk) to discover a space said to be home to ghostly bibliophiles. Books flying off shelves and long-dead professors walking between the volumes are just two pieces of paranormal action logged here.

After such ghostly encounters, it's perhaps time to relax in one of the city's great watering holes. But maybe think twice about going in the Bear Inn if you're of a nervous disposition; there's a spectre here who suddenly vanishes, and objects have been known to move around on their own. The Turf Tavern, meanwhile, is said to be haunted by 'Old Rosie', a former barmaid who moves cutlery and taps patrons on the shoulder. Get to know a whole haunted house worth of other Oxford spirits on one of the city's ghost tours (www.theoxfordghosttour.co.uk), and give my regards to the Broad Street ghosts.

BROAD STREET, OXFORD, OX1 3BJ

34 Gloucester Prison, Gloucestershire

Inside this clink with a grim reputation you'll find plenty of opportunities to probe the paranormal and test your nerve

This once-fearsome prison – now home to some terrifying ghostly experiences – was built on the site of the Norman-era Gloucester Castle, the keep of which was at one time used to house convicted criminals. Opening as the county jail towards the end of the 18th century, it was added to as recently as the 1980s. But the prison gained a reputation for overcrowding, tough conditions and prisoner protests before its eventual closure in 2013, and the centuries of misery on this site have caused many a tormented soul to linger long into the afterlife, meaning it now has a reputation for the paranormal and attracts those visitors seeking ghostly goings-on.

One of Gloucester Prison's most popular events is Investigator Night, during which the doors to the prison are thrown open and paranormal enthusiasts invited inside to conduct their own investigations. There's plenty of room to accommodate a number of groups, giving you and your team of ghost hunters the opportunity to have a room all to yourself while you carry out your own tests into the spooky occurrences. The prison actively encourages you to bring along your own supernatural recording

ABOVE Have you the courage to conduct your own ghost hunt at Gloucester Prison and livestream it?

equipment and to take as many images as you like in hopes of capturing a spectre on film. Maybe you'll broadcast the entire evening's events live on TikTok, bringing chills to a much larger audience. In the past, these evenings have even thrown up spooky sounds like footsteps and sudden, unexplained whistles.

Talking about scary things, can you imagine playing hide and seek inside the prison? We all liked to play the game as kids, but could you stomach it in such a spooky environment – in the pitch-black, not knowing who (or what) might be lurking round every corner? Well, the prison also hosts an event called Gloucester Hide & Seek and it's one of the most frightening experiences you can take part in. As the seeker counts to 100, 60 hiders must dash off to find a shadowy nook or creepy cranny in which to hide. But will your nerves stand the test?

The guide leading this tour takes you to all the paranormal hotspots: the places that have received the most frequent reports of activity over the decades. The five execution sites are especially fascinating. A total of 123 people were executed on this site for a range of crimes, the last of them in 1939. Many of them remain buried here in unmarked graves. Naturally, then, there are many reasons for spirits to hold grudges and wallow here in their tormented state.

This is not a place to be taken lightly. But should you decide you're brave enough to book a tour, you're advised to wrap up warm. The prison can get cold at night, especially when you feel an unexpected chilly air that will make your hair stand on end…

BARRACK SQUARE, GLOUCESTER, GLOUCESTERSHIRE, GL1 2JN
WWW.GLOUCESTER-PRISON.CO.UK

35 Royal Shakespeare Theatre Ghost Tour, Stratford-upon-Avon, Warwickshire

Take an after-hours tour around the theatre to hear about spooky happenings both on and off stage

The birthplace of the Bard is a great place to learn about weird phenomena and mysterious hauntings linked to thespians treading the boards. How could a town connected with such petrifying plays as *Hamlet* and *Macbeth* not have a few creepy tales to tell? For those directors wanting their productions to be as realistic and chilling as possible, creating the ghosts of Hamlet's father and Banquo on stage can be a challenge. Actors, too, are generally incredibly superstitious types, which gives the productions an even more eerie aspect. And when you throw in a few supernatural sightings, it's clear why theatres are thought by some paranormal investigators to be among the most active buildings when it comes to supernatural activity.

Ghosts appear in five Shakespeare plays, and the world-famous playwright used them to great effect, especially when combined with stunning costumes, make-up and sounds. Some are gory, some are silent, sometimes we're not sure if they're meant to be real or in a character's head, but they always have an important impact on the narrative. The spectres at the Royal Shakespeare Theatre, however, are not limited to those appearing on the

BELOW Ghosts have appeared on stage and backstage at Stratford.

stage. Down the generations, apparitions have been witnessed by actors and support staff while they are backstage. The 'Grey Lady' has been spotted many times wandering around the theatre's corridors, while cold spots have been reported too. Perhaps most telling is the feeling of being watched. Actors are used to being scrutinised by audience and critics, but some have told of an oppressive and sometimes overwhelming sense of being observed by an invisible presence.

Now here's another spooky aspect. The acting profession is riddled with superstition. Performers are told to 'break a leg' because they think saying 'good luck' will act as a curse and cause them to come to harm. And while witchcraft features predominantly in *Macbeth*, theatre professionals avoid saying its name, instead referring to it as the 'Scottish Play', due to its association with disaster and bad luck. (Don't worry, it's OK to read it. I think.) 'Bad things' occurred right from the Scottish play's first staging: James I banned it because he didn't like it, and legend has it that one of the first women to play Lady Macbeth died right before a performance, meaning Shakespeare himself had to step in to replace her. Actors have been injured when real knives were used instead of props. During the Old Vic's 1937 production, Laurence Olivier was nearly killed by a falling stage weight, while both director and actor playing Lady Macbeth were injured in a car crash.

ABOVE Four candles good, three candles bad: the theatre is rife with superstition.

Elsewhere in theatre lore, it's also deemed bad luck to bring peacock feathers and mirrors onto the stage, as well as use real money and/or jewellery. As for lighting three candles at once in a performance, well; you'd be considered by many to be crazy! You'll find all this out and more on the brilliant after-hours tour of the Royal Shakespeare Theatre, so settle in for a seriously spooky show.

WATERSIDE, STRATFORD-UPON-AVON, WARWICKSHIRE, CV37 6BB
WWW.RSC.ORG.UK

36 Warwick Castle, Warwickshire

Step into medieval times and you may glimpse some of the centuries-old ghosts rumoured still to linger here

Sitting on the banks of the River Avon, Warwick Castle is one of the most complete examples of a medieval fortress in Britain. It's history spans more than a thousand years, it's been at the centre of several important battles, and today it pulls in tourists from around the world looking to enjoy a day of thrilling events, including falconry displays, archery practice and storytelling – not forgetting the rare chance to see a full-size trebuchet fire its fiery load towards the enemy. At this family-friendly attraction you'll find costumed actors and guides amid incredibly well-preserved architecture. But it's not all fun, for this has been the site of many a macabre event down the centuries, from battles to torture. As such, it's a hotbed of paranormal activity and supernatural sightings are well documented here. So whose are the most frequent apparitions?

One of Warwick Castle's most famous ghosts belongs to poet and royal courtier Sir Fulke Greville. Great name, isn't it? He was granted the castle in 1604 and spent a fortune restoring it before being stabbed by his servant on a trip to London, dying weeks later due to the infection that resulted. You're most likely to come across his spirit in the tower that is named after him; several visitors and staff have spoken of cold drafts and a sudden melancholy descending upon them within its walls. Some have even seen his spectral figure wandering the

RIGHT You may emerge from the dungeons looking like you've seen a ghost.

halls in Elizabethan clothing. Chillingly, he's also been spotted hanging around his own portrait. But his killer, Ralph Heywood, did not get away scot-free. Feeling immense regret and remorse, he took his own life immediately after committing the crime, and died before his master. Some ghost hunters reckon Heywood's spirit is trapped inside the castle to this day.

Guy of Warwick is another legendary figure of medieval England, said to be both a heroic knight and a slayer of great beasts. Sounds like a good Guy. His ghost is reported to appear in the Great Hall, as he watches over visitors from within his armoured suit. Other knights are also known to clank around the castle, though not all of them have been identified. Perhaps they are the ghosts of warriors who died in battle and cannot leave the place they were defending until their untimely end. It must be quite a sight seeing a ghostly suit of armour rattling down the old corridors.

BELOW Warwick Castle is one of the best preserved in the land.

However, the spookiest experience is reserved for those who happen across the ghosts of children within the castle walls. There are thought to be quite a few of them, among them the offspring of noblemen or servants who perished for one reason or another when they were young. Tiny footsteps running free on the floors and creepy children's laughter have been reported, and occasionally chilling child-like spectres have been seen playing here.

For many, the most disturbing part of a trip to Warwick Castle is a journey to the dungeon, where you'll get to see where all centuries of torture and imprisonment took place, itself said to be a place where spirits are rife. But wherever you venture within this incredible building, you'll be walking through rooms said to be haunted by centuries-old ghosts. And not all of them are friendly...

CASTLE LANE, WARWICK, WARWICKSHIRE, CV34 4QU
WWW.WARWICK-CASTLE.COM

37 The Bone Crypt at Holy Trinity Church, Rothwell, Northamptonshire

Discover the bones of thousands in this dark but thought-provoking crypt

Rothwell is a small town in Northamptonshire, established by the Vikings under the name 'Rodewell' and currently home to a population of around 7,000. But this settlement is perhaps best known for its non-living population – the 2,500 souls that lie in the crypt beneath Rothwell's Holy Trinity Church. Research suggests the bone crypt dates back to the 13th century, the ancient nature of these remains somehow adding to the eerie feeling as you descend from the church. This is one of only two such macabre crypts in the country – the other being at St Leonard's in Hythe, which is also featured in this book (page 40). Together, they make a pair of creepy afternoons out, walking among the dead on display.

RIGHT Sunday skulls: make sure you plan your visit for when the crypt is open.
OPPOSITE The skull collection at Rothwell can be unnerving.

Local legend has it that nothing was known about the crypt until one day, in the 18th century, a man employed as a gravedigger fell into it while he was working in the church. Clueless about its existence, the gravedigger suddenly found himself far beneath the church, in the dark and surrounded by nothing but human bones. Naturally, this would have been a traumatic experience, and it certainly took its toll on the church employee, who is said to have been driven mad by the incident, scarred by the deathly discovery until his dying day. The bones are no longer strewn around like they were back then; they have since been carefully reorganised and meticulously displayed on specially built shelving along the walls, while there are two large square piles of thigh bones in the centre of the room.

As for where the bones come from, there have been many theories put forward over the years. Were they Danes killed in in a bitter fight? How about soldiers killed in a 1645 battle at Naseby? Or are they the victims of a plague epidemic? Science has kicked all these thoughts into touch, though. The skulls don't show signs of battle, while plague victims were unlikely to be buried beneath the actual church. Time to call in researchers from the University of Sheffield, then. Their investigations revealed the bodies in the crypt came from a range of different periods, from medieval days right up to the year 1900. It's likely the bones at Rothwell were accumulated over centuries simply to make room in the churchyard for the recently deceased. And as for why the collection is made up solely of skulls and femurs, well that's linked to early Christian beliefs that these were the only things needed for resurrection. As long as you had the skull and femur, God would be able to find all the missing bits and fix you up.

Make sure you don't just turn up and expect to get into this fascinating space: opening times are limited to Sundays, after the church service, and visitor numbers are restricted due to space. So, you're recommended to book in advance through the email contact on the church's website. Be prepared to be amazed at what is both a shocking and humbling experience, not to mention a very rare one on these shores.

HOLY TRINITY CHURCH, SQUIRES HILL, ROTHWELL, KETTERING, NORTHAMPTONSHIRE, NN14 6BQ
WWW.ROTHWELLHOLYTRINITY.ORG.UK

38 The Coffin Works, Birmingham

Spend an afternoon in this eerie city-centre museum, formerly a factory making coffins to house the dead

There can be few city-centre buildings that have such a spooky vibe as Birmingham's Coffin Works. You'll find this former Victorian factory tucked away in the famous Jewellery Quarter, looming behind a set of 19th-century gates, and there's no doubt at all that this place is dripping with creepy vibes. Of course it is; this is a factory built on a profitable but macabre business, at a time when Victorians were obsessed with all things dead or dying. The building is now a museum that marks the craftsmanship of the people who worked here and the positive role they played for the recently bereaved. It is also one of the strangest, darkest places to spend an afternoon, and yet there is much to be learnt here – and even celebrated. Even though the shadow of death is never far away, it's as fascinating as it is unsettling.

Producing some of the finest coffins in the world, this factory was opened in 1882 by brothers Alfred and Edwin Newman. Initially they were brass founders and made cabinets, but they soon found a niche market for producing high-class funerary goods. Coffin handles, urns, linings, shrouds – it was all made here and assembled into the coffin, the final resting place for many of us. Known for their high standards, the Newman Brothers produced the coffin furniture for some very important British figures, including Winston Churchill, Joseph Chamberlain, the Queen Mother and Princess Diana.

ABOVE Machinery from the factory is still on display.
OPPOSITE The Coffin Works, a factory that decorated many a Victorian casket.

Business boomed here until the end of the 20th century, when a reluctance to adopt modern methods and the banning of metal parts on coffins used for cremations led to the company's decline. The end came quickly, and the factory was left in a state of sudden abandonment in 1998. After a period of disuse, the building was reopened as one of the country's most unusual museums in 2014. Walking around the museum you get a sense of the care that went into creating these products and, indeed, the care at the heart of the funerary business. You'll learn the industry hit a turning point in the 1930s, when the job of 'undertaker' became that of 'funeral director', and the Newman Brothers built on this newfound respect to become market leaders. The museum is a well-preserved window into their world, how well they treated death as a sensitive subject and how the factory looked in the 1960s.

Underlining everything at this former factory is the fact that death is actually big business. Although those experiencing the loss of a loved one may be suffering immensely, many jobs and businesses depend on people passing away. Figures vary year on year, but on average a 600,000 people die in the UK every year. The average cost of a burial is now nearly £5,000, and the funeral industry is worth well over £2.5 billion annually. Behind every terrible tale in this book or spooky attraction, there is the potential for economic gain. The Newman Brothers, who at one time were one of the most important employers in Birmingham, clearly delivered this service in a most tasteful and skilful way.

FLEET STREET, JEWELLERY QUARTER, BIRMINGHAM, B3 1JP
WWW.COFFINWORKS.ORG

39 Dudley Castle, West Midlands

Visit the popular Dudley Castle and explore its fascinating history while you search for the famous ghost of the Grey Lady

With origins going back to the 11th century, work began on Dudley Castle as we know it today in 1537, under the instruction of John Dudley, a man soon to rise through the royal ranks and become Duke of Northumberland, part of the Regency Council supervising the nine-year-old King Edward VI (r. 1547–53). Dudley Castle grew as a fortress and was visited by Queen Elizabeth I in 1575, and was later used by Royalist troops during the English Civil War and was besieged in 1644 and 1646. A century later, in 1750, a three-day blaze ripped through the Sharington Range buildings near the castle and the building fell into ruin. Then, in 1937, there was a change of direction when the Earl of Dudley opened a zoo displaying animals from around the world. Dudley Zoo remains a popular attraction to this day, and with the kind of bloody history it boasts it's hardly surprising the castle's ghost tours are also incredibly popular.

Some ghost-hunting experts claim Dudley Castle is the most haunted castle in England. It's certainly up there with the scariest of them. A wide range of spirits have been spotted on this site and linked to historical events from its rich past. But most unusual is that some have actually been *captured on camera*. You read that right: this is one of the very few places claiming to have strong visual evidence of the spooks living there. The viral sensation occurred in 2021, when a cyclist went around the grounds as he captured images for Google Street View and managed to snap a mysterious, dark figure in one of the windows. Search for it online. It's certainly an interesting sight.

BELOW The Castle on the hill: could you be the next person to capture a spirit on film?

That same year, a visitor claimed to have captured the ghost of a little drumming boy in a photo. Compelling stuff.

Some years earlier, another tourist took a photo of the castle, but when you zoom in to one of the doors, you can see what looks to be the 'Grey Lady'.

Several female spectres in this book have been named after the colour dress they posthumously rock up in, and there's more than one Grey Lady. But given the national media attention given to the one residing in Dudley Castle, this ghost has had more than its 15 minutes of fame. According to paranormal experts, this is the apparition of Lady Dorothy Beaumont, wife of a colonel stationed at the castle during the English Civil War. Lady Dorothy gave birth to a child in 1644, which sadly died on the same day and was buried in a churchyard outside the castle walls. A further morose twist in the tale came when Lady Dorothy died sometime later. Her dying wish was to be buried alongside her child in that same churchyard. But the war was still raging and the castle was under siege, making it impossible to fulfil her request, and she was laid to rest within the castle walls. Separated from her offspring in the afterlife, it's thought this is the reason her frustrated soul stills roams the castle's ruins.

If you don't spot the Grey Lady then maybe you'll see the ghost of John de Somery, who died in 1322 and is said to be buried beneath the castle's chapel. Or maybe it will be spooky sounds you hear; these are often linked to the terrible fire that tore through the castle in the 18th century and they come in the form of cries and screams. Others have reported seeing a flickering light in darkened areas, as if the flames from that blaze are trapped between that day and this. The team from *Most Haunted* have even been here to check out these paranormal claims, while several tourists visiting the attraction to see monkeys and lions have gone home with much more of a spooky experience than they bargained for.

CASTLE HILL, DUDLEY, WEST MIDLANDS, DY1 4QF
WWW.DUDLEYZOO.ORG.UK/DUDLEY-CASTLE

40 Cannock Chase, Staffordshire

Some say this beautiful countryside makes for a great day out, while others liken it to Area 51...

A fabulous asset for communities living nearby, the National Landscape that is Cannock Chase holds a wealth of outdoor opportunities for those wanting to have fun in the countryside. With hiking, biking, horse-riding, fishing and potential to delve into the area's rich history, Cannock Chase is a very popular place to spend a day out. On sunny days, at any rate; having read up about the diverse spirits linked to this neck of the woods, I wouldn't like to be here at dusk, or even when the drizzle and mist roll in across the heathland. For Cannock Chase is renowned for its strange hauntings. So, come here for the day. Bring a picnic if you wish. But no matter how much fun you have, you're bound to spend some time wondering just what is lurking in the middle of those woods...

The best-known of Cannock Chase's ghostly legends involves the 'Black-Eyed Child', an apparition that sounds as fearsome as any I've head about. Witnesses claim to have seen a young figure with pale skin and, what's worse, large black voids where their eyes should be. Several people passing through – often lone walkers or drivers – say they've seen the ghostly child wandering through these woods, then vanishing without a trace after a few moments. Some say the Black-Eyed Child is the long-dead victim of disease or murder.

ABOVE What's that amongst the trees? The black-eyed girl? Or the Pig Man?
OPPOSITE Arriving in the area on a misty day will make it even more chilling.

There is certainly no shortage of sightings; recent news articles claim the ghostly child has been snooping around campers, and one ghost hunter reckons he photographed the child with his drone. Check it out online. The footage looks like the girl from *The Ring*, and I would very much like to avoid coming across her during a walk in the woods.

If spooky kids with black eyes aren't bad enough, you may also come face to face with the 'Lady in White'. Gliding through the trees at Castle Ring – an Iron

Age fort – and wearing a long, flowing white gown, she is reported by many who have seen her to convey an overwhelming sense of sorrow. Maybe she came to a sorry end. We will never know.

Seeing a ghost is one thing, but Cannock Chase has developed a reputation for many other types of paranormal activity that put it in a different league to other spooky settings on our shores. In fact, the chase has even been compared with Roswell and Area 51 in the United States – there's that much unexplained stuff going down here. Entire books have been written about the mysteries of Cannock Chase, which include shape-shifting entities and UFOs. However, by far the most terrifying in my opinion is the so-called 'Pig-Man', who's said to live near Pye Green Tower. This beast has the body of a human man and – you guessed it – the head of a pig. Sightings of the Cannock Chase Pig-Man date back to the Second World War, with some folk reckoning the creature to be the result of a local scientific experiment gone badly wrong. Instead of creating super soldiers, they made a Pig-Man, who somehow made it into the wild. I guess it's typical, really; the United States' Second World War super soldier ends up being the legendary Captain America and we end up with a half-man, half-pig wandering woods in the Midlands. It might all be porkies, of course, but some locals swear they've seen this swine in the trees, grunting. They'll probably see snout like it again.

POPULAR CAR PARK AT BIRCHES VALLEY, RUGELEY, WS15 2UQ

41 Grave of the Last Sin-Eater, St Mary's Church, Ratlinghope, Shropshire

Explore the final resting place of a man paid to absorb the wrongdoings of others

In times when the people of the UK were far more God-fearing, being buried without first confessing your sins was a big deal. It could literally affect where you ended up spending eternity. Revealing one's wrongdoings on one's deathbed became something of a priority for the terminally ill. Sometimes, though, it just couldn't be done, and that's where the 'sin-eater' came into play. Sin-eaters (which, admittedly sound like something straight from *Harry Potter*) were people who thought nothing of selling their soul to the devil and absorbing the misdemeanours of those who had passed on. The ritual, performed to rid the dead of their sins, involved the sin-eater being handed a simple meal across the coffin. They would then consume it, thereby symbolically taking on board the dead person's sins and absolving them of their sins. The ritual varied across the country, but typically it involved the sin-eater

ABOVE It's a sin, and this guy used to eat them for breakfast.

receiving bread and wine or beer to eat, while a payment would also be handed over in exchange for the dark service being provided. Historians can't say how common sin-eating was across the UK, but it seems regions along the England–Wales border were a particular hotspot.

And that's why we turn our attention to the quiet Shropshire village of Ratlinghope. In St Margaret's churchyard you'll find a small, unassuming marker for the grave of Richard Munslow – Britain's last sin-eater, who died in 1906. Munslow bucked the trend when it came to consuming the sins of the dead because he was a wealthy farmer and didn't fit the usual socioeconomic profile of your usual sin-eater. Many of those carrying out this otherworldly ritual were poor vagrants, probably more concerned about where the next meal was coming from than whether or not they were going to make it to heaven. Records speak of sin-eaters living in isolation, being treated with hostility and only being called upon when somebody died without confessing their sins. Even the wooden plates they used in the ritual were often burned after they'd used them. Sadly, in the case of Richard Munslow, it's thought he may have revived the old tradition out of desperation when three of his children died of scarlet fever within a week in 1870.

There's evidence sin-eating also took place in nearby Market Drayton as late as 1893, while similar rituals occurred in other European countries. In parts of Germany, for example, a corpse cake was set upon the chest of the deceased and then eaten by the nearest relative. Dutch 'dead cakes' had the initials of the departed person written on them and were handed out to those attending the funeral (these were later introduced to the United States). And in the Balkans during the 19th century, pieces of bread were made in the image of the deceased and eaten by family members. In the UK, the tradition of serving funeral biscuits and burial cakes is thought to have evolved from the practice of sin-eating, a macabre funeral tradition that came to an end with the burial of Richard Munslow here in quiet Ratlinghope.

RATLINGHOPE, SHREWSBURY, SHROPSHIRE, SY5 0SR

42 Shrewsbury Prison, Shropshire

Experience the thrills and chills of a spooky ghost tour in a haunted prison

A prison has stood on this site since 1793 and inmates were holed up here as recently as 2013. Throughout that time there have inevitably been many unpleasant happenings inside these walls. No wonder, then, that paranormal experts consider Shrewsbury Prison to be haunted by a number of spirits. In fact, the site has gained a global reputation. Now open as a tourist attraction, school groups and other visitors come here during the day to find out what conditions were like inside the old prison – and to have a go at a cracking escape room experience, in which you literally have to break out of a sealed cell. After dark, though, the prison becomes a very different place – not somewhere you'd want to be on your own if you are fearful of the supernatural. The Victorian prison you see standing today was built on top of a Georgian prison, and both had some very unsavoury people passing through the gate.

Some prisoners never left again. In the 20th century alone, eight people were hanged here for the crime of murder. Two were killed in a brick shed at the back of the site, while later an execution room was created near the front. Each of the hanged men were buried on site

ABOVE Will you be able to escape the prison?
OPPOSITE Take a tour, but beware the poltergeist room in the prison.

in unmarked graves, as was the custom. Four executions in the 1950s were carried out by well-known hangman Albert Pierrepoint, who is thought to have hanged up to 600 people during his career. Oh yes, this building harbours many miserable memories and housed men who had done unspeakable things. Book an evening ghost tour and you're taken deep into this world, so be prepared to be properly creeped out.

The tour lasts 90 minutes and is suitable for over-12s only (even the more nervous among us may find some of the details rather shocking). My own daughter visited the prison on a school trip during her A-levels and three of the group passed out during the introduction. They were told that wasn't uncommon.

The tour starts off at the Georgian Gate Lodge, the historic entrance, before heading into the most haunted part of the prison, C Wing. Here you'll hear tales of the Grey Lady, a ghostly figure that has been seen walking the landings at night. More terrifying still is learning about the small Georgian boy known to appear on a particular set of steps.

If you're still fit to continue with the tour after all this, things start to hot up when you move into A Wing, home of the infamous 'Shadow Man'. Often seen watching the tour groups from a doorway at the end of the wing, it's thought the Shadow Man died on that very spot.

There'll also be time for you to wander around the prison by torchlight, and an opportunity for you to be shut in a cell, if you're brave enough. But be warned: it's pitch black with the door closed and a deafening silence grips you. As you explore the prison on your own, you may want to avoid going to Cell 210. Known as the Poltergeist Cell, one former occupant is still reckoned to be trapped inside. Several visitors have been caught unawares in there, some describing being forced out of the cell as though they were trespassing. Legend has it that some wardens refused to go in there, too. So, tread carefully.

THE DANA, SHREWSBURY,
SHROPSHIRE, SY1 2HP
WWW.SHREWSBURYPRISON.COM

43 Hack Green Secret Nuclear Bunker, Cheshire

Head underground into what would have been the command centre for political and military leaders if World War Three had started

The threat of nuclear war was very real from the 1960s to the 1980s. The plan in the corridors of power was to house the regional leaders of northern England in this Cheshire underground bunker were an attack ever launched from the Soviet Union. Just how creepy you find this relatively new attraction depends on whether you were alive during the Cold War. If you're too young to remember President Reagan's sword rattling or Kennedy's Cuban missile crisis, what you find below the surface at Hack Green may seem like the film set and props from a dystopian film. But if you're old enough to have lived through it, and if you can recall the chilling public information bulletins and the genuine fear among the population, this is going to be a whole lot more disturbing.

Building here started in the 1950s when a secret radar network was established at the beginning of the Arms Race. By 1984, there was a 3,251 sq. m (35,000 sq. ft) command and control centre in operation. It remained ready for action until 1993, when the frosty Cold War relations had thawed. In 1998, the site was opened to the public and immediately became one of the country's most unusual and macabre tourist attractions. Visitors can see gas masks issued at the time, radiation suits that would have been worn were the attack to take place and the medical room equipped to deal with horrific injuries.

But the creepiest of all the items on display at the bunker are the nuclear weapons themselves, and there's quite a

ABOVE Getting scared in this chilling place doesn't mean you're a dummy.
OPPOSITE No longer a secret, this Cold War bunker is open for all.

collection of them. Secret negotiations took place between the bunker and high levels of government in the late 1990s, resulting in the dismantling and transportation to the bunker of the last remaining WE 177 nuclear weapons and more besides. They were moved to Cheshire in an unmarked RAF transport and installed in the bunker when it was closed to the public. Few people have got up close to these weapons of mass destruction. They're now perfectly safe, having been dismantled, but if detonated over a Russian city they would have killed unthinkable numbers of people in an instant. To be close to one of these weapons is indeed a strange experience.

If the actual existence of a nuclear bunker isn't scary enough, how about we throw in a ghost or two? There have been several sightings inside this bunker, and it's perhaps not surprising that some souls are trapped in here, given the nature of the building. A ghostly man dressed in a uniform has been seen in the main corridor. Staff have reported feeling a disturbing concentration of energy in the area. The communications room is also thought to house a spook or two, with some paranormal groups spotting a young woman working at a desk and others reporting the disconnected old telephones suddenly ringing on their own. The most activity has been recorded in the theatre, where visitors have been pushed and felt an overwhelming sickness. One of the tours organised by Haunted Rooms (www.hauntedrooms.co.uk) had a woman so badly affected that an ambulance had to be called.

Hack Green is available to hire for paranormal investigations and it's possible to book onto tours organised by professional ghost hunters if you check online for details.

FRENCH LN, NANTWICH, CW5 8BL
WWW.HACKGREEN.CO.UK

44 National Justice Museum, Nottingham

Delve into the history of crime and punishment, but watch out for some of the spirits it left behind

A thoroughly good afternoon out, the National Justice Museum can be found in the Grade II listed Shire Hall in Nottingham's Lace Market district. There are five floors to discover, each documenting the history of crime, punishment and social justice. Inside you'll find a Victorian courtroom, a Georgian jail and cells that housed prisoners hundreds of years ago. You'll find out about the jailers, judges and prisoners who spent time here – some staying longer than others, some never leaving. There's an emphasis on bringing the past to life at the museum, so expect to see people in costumes playing the role of local historical figures. The thing that sticks in the memory of many visitors is the re-enactment of a historical trial, giving you a taste of what it was like to attend a public execution.

What went on within these walls was horrendous. Treatment of prisoners was often brutal. Some were condemned to death and executed right here. Others spent many years locked up in desperate conditions. Unsurprisingly, it's become a much visited haunt for paranormal investigators, with many in agreement that this old hall is home to several trapped spirits who were badly treated here. Shadowy figures moving within

BELOW Any last words? Rough justice was handed out here to some.

and between the prison cells have been reported by many and a common sighting is of an old, thin man in ragged clothing. He's thought to be a former inmate who died on the inside. Look out for him – some say he stares out of the cell between the iron bars, vanishing when approached.

In the former judges' chambers, you may feel an ominous presence, an oppressive feeling of authority. Tourists claim to have heard his gavel striking wood. Miscarriages of justice were rife in centuries gone by, and one such wrongly convicted woman seen moving through the courtroom is now known as the 'Woman in White'. Some say she looks incredibly sorrowful, sometimes crying and trying to whisper without being able to make a sound. Many spirits in these chambers are unhappy ones who struggled through very difficult times.

The Galleries of Justice – as the buildings here are known – were the only location in the UK where you could go through the entire process of trial, sentencing and execution. You could be put on trial in the courts here, and if found guilty the judge would pass down the sentence. If the suitable punishment was deemed to be hanging, then that could also be dealt with here too. It was, for sure, a miserable place. Some of the hangings took place on the steps outside so crowds could gather to witness the event. Sometimes the gatherings were large and unruly.

Check out the museum website, or www.hauntedhappenings.co.uk, for details on the ghost nights held here, which are carried out with professional paranormal hunters running an event into the early hours. Those brave enough to take part in these evenings have reported extreme drops in temperatures and screams coming from within the building. On rare occasions, journeys down to the caves beneath the prison have had terrifying consequences, with horrendous noises being witnessed and strange lights being picked up on cameras. You have been warned…

HIGH PAVEMENT, NOTTINGHAM, NG1 1HN
WWW.NATIONALJUSTICEMUSEUM.ORG.UK

45 Ye Olde Trip to Jerusalem, Nottingham

Buy a pint at this ancient inn and you may get a ghost and a curse thrown in as a side order

Try claiming to know the location of Britain's oldest pub and there'll be a handful of other ancient hostelries queuing up to shoot you down. Suggest that your own local is the most haunted pub in the country and there'll be a *Ghostbusters* van-load of others who claim to have plenty of their own things that go bump in the night. So, without making wild claims, let's just agree that if you visit Ye Olde Trip to Jerusalem in the centre of Nottingham you'll be entering a pub that is *very old*. And *very haunted*. The owners of the curiously named Ye Olde Trip to Jerusalem say the doors to the bar first opened in 1189. It's a fascinating building, full of little nooks

and crannies that provide plenty of places for you to stow away with a beer – and lots of hangouts for ghosts. The pub is built into the bottom of Castle Rock, literally sticking out of the huge piece of bedrock that houses the castle high above.

There are many stories and legends associated with Ye Olde Trip to Jerusalem, dating back to the days of Robin Hood, the Sherrif of Nottingham and Richard the Lionheart. It was also a rest point for people who had begun their journey to the Holy Land, either on crusades or pilgrimages, and this is why it adopted the name it did. Those early decades of operation saw beer brewed here for those residing within the castle's walls, with a pulley system transporting the goods to the top of the rock. Today, it's on the city's tourist trail, a good place to eat and drink with an ideal photo opportunity outside, as writing on the wall declares just how old it is.

Wherever you sit in the pub, you're unlikely to be far away from a fascinating story about a spirit or a curse. The place is dripping with them. One of the most famous sightings is of a man called George H. Ward, better known as 'Yorkey'. He's been seen many times sitting in the lounge that was affectionately named after him. Some say he's even prone to playing practical jokes on those who've come in the bar for a pint. Making loud

noises and pulling on people's clothes are common japes in his repertoire, things that wouldn't be out of character when he was alive, some locals say.

Another spook spotted in the pub is known as the 'Figure in Black'. Exactly who is this customer from the afterlife? Nobody is sure, but it could be a knight that was stripped of his title for being badly behaved – they were called black knights. Either way, this tall, dark shadow of a person rushes around scaring the bejeebies out of drinkers.

For me, though, the creepiest part of the pub has nothing to do with ghosts – it's a curse. Upstairs, in the Rock Lounge, safely placed in a glass case, you'll find the Cursed Galleon – an old, dirty, dusty antique model of a ship. The origins have been lost in time, but it's been in the pub for 300 years and used to hang near the bar. But here's the thing – when people have tried to clean it they have been struck down by misfortune. One landlord died within a year of dusting it down. Two other landlords died much sooner when they attempted to give it a polish. A cleaner had the idea of taking it down, sprucing it up and placing it in protective casing; she too passed away within weeks. One legend reckons a witch had beef with the pub and placed a curse on anybody touching the galleon. You may or may not believe in the curse of the galleon, but I for one gave it a wide berth.

BREWHOUSE YARD, NOTTINGHAM, NG1 6AD
WWW.GREENEKING.CO.UK/PUBS/NOTTINGHAMSHIRE/YE-OLDE-TRIP-TO-JERUSALEM

ABOVE Solid as a rock, the pub is literally built into the cliff.
RIGHT Spooky goings-on have been described throughout this old pub.

46 The Workhouse, Southwell, Nottinghamshire

Tourists now visit this building that once housed the Victorian poor, but are there other things lurking here too?

You would be forgiven for thinking that Southwell Workhouse is merely an impressive building in pleasant surroundings, but take a tour around this imposing site and you'll discover a grim history beyond its wall. The workhouse was built in 1824 to provide shelter, food and hard labour for those at the very bottom of Victorian society's harsh hierarchy. As many as 160 men, women and children were based here at any one time, all of whom were kept in bleak conditions and put to work on tasks such as grinding up bones to make fertiliser. Today, the building, run by the National Trust and open to visitors, remains the best example of a Victorian workhouse, and it offers a powerful insight into 19th-century attitudes towards the destitute – most of which were not good. The men and women who lived here were segregated, while the food was grim and in short supply. With so much suffering and unhappiness, it's inevitable there are many supernatural stories.

When you step inside the workhouse, you'll find yourself peering into bare rooms and traversing down long, draughty corridors, once the scene

RIGHT Listen out for footsteps as you wander the corridors.
BELOW The ghosts of yesteryear have been seen at Southwell.

of some very heavy, disheartened footsteps. Will you be one of the visitors to wander along them and report seeing shadowy figures? Dark silhouettes have been spotted looming large at the end of the corridors, only to vanish when approached. Is this a trick of the light or the lingering spectres of people who came here as a result of the Poor Law? Perhaps they are bewildered as to why such an awful place is now a tourist attraction?

Many tears have been shed in the workhouse by those in a less fortunate position than the visitors paying for entry today. The heartbreaking sobs of a young boy or girl have been heard coming from the living quarters, a reminder of how distressing life could be here for those young people separated from their families and put through such hardship. The ghost of a man and a woman have also been seen wandering the corridors, as if looking for each other.

The workhouse yard, so confined and with the imposing walls of the huge building bearing down on it, is the place where inhabitants – awkwardly referred to as the 'inmates' – were allowed out for their daily exercise, much like a prison. Ghostly, misty apparitions have been spotted here, sometimes trudging around in endless circles. Will you hear the shuffling of feet?

Rumours also circulate about what's going on in the attic, which is riddled with trauma but also disturbingly fascinating. Recordings have been made that claim to capture whispering voices from long ago, and some noises that cannot be explained. Visiting the workhouse in a group or with a friend is one thing. Being left in such chilling places on your own, well that's something else entirely.

UPTON RD, SOUTHWELL, NG25 0PT
WWW.NATIONALTRUST.ORG.UK/VISIT/NOTTINGHAMSHIRE-LINCOLNSHIRE/THE-WORKHOUSE-AND-INFIRMARY

47 Lincoln Castle, Lincolnshire

Visit the prison that kept all of its inmates in isolation and drove many to madness

With a formidable Norman castle and an impressive cathedral dating back to the 11th century, Lincoln is truly one of the great English cities and has history running through its veins. Every street in the centre of this east of England treasure has stories to tell, of Civil War encounters, visits by kings and queens, political upheaval. Many grim and gruesome events unfolded here, meaning Lincoln has more than its fair share of ghostly tales, too. Any paranormal investigator worth their salt will put Lincoln high up the list of Britain's most haunted locations. And if you're wanting to dip your toe into this spooky city, there's only one place to start your journey. And that's the castle.

ABOVE Lincoln Castle has an incredible history.

William the Conqueror gave the order to build Lincoln Castle in 1068 and it has stood proudly ever since. Famously, this iconic building is home to an original version of the Magna Carta. Perched on a hill in the centre of the city, Lincoln Castle has operated as not only a symbol of strategic power for the best part of a thousand years, but also a keeper of justice. With such a long history through some traumatic periods, it's no surprise to discover many a macabre event taking place within these walls. And the spiritual impacts linger on down the generations.

It's widely accepted that one of the most haunted parts of the castle is the Victorian prison, which kept inmates in brutal conditions for decades starting from 1848. Those banged up in cells were subjected to the 'separate system', which kept them in isolation. This was intended to make the prisoners reflect, repent and reform. In reality, it had an incredibly detrimental effect on their mental health, something not understood at all in Victorian times. Several died in the prison and were buried on site. Others were driven insane by their time alone. As a result, this inhumane prison has a sorrowful feel to it. Visitors have reported feeling sudden cold spots in and around the cells. Mournful crying has also been heard. It's not a place you'd like to spend the night alone, although there is the chance to experience the isolation of a cell for a few moments of solitary confinement. And that's quite enough, thank you. Away from the prison, the castle's burial area and the location for public hangings have also been said to have given visitors the heebie-jeebies.

Aside from the castle, you should still be on alert for spooky happenings in nearby streets. The Battle of Lincoln in 1217 left many dead soldiers both inside and outside the castle walls. Some visitors claim to have heard cries, listened to traumatised voices and felt like they were being watched intently. For a spooky walk around other parts of the city, visit www.lincolnghostwalks.co.uk and book a session that will explore lots of local legends in a 90-minute bonanza of creepy storytelling.

CASTLE HILL, LINCOLN, LN1 3AA
WWW.LINCOLNCASTLE.COM

BELOW The streets of Lincoln are as ghostly and atmospheric as any you will find.

The North

48 **Creswell Crags,** Worksop, Nottinghamshire
49 **Lyceum Theatre,** Sheffield, South Yorkshire
50 **Eyam,** Derbyshire
51 **Little John's Grave,** St Michael's Church, Hathersage, Derbyshire
52 **Winnats Pass,** Castleton, Derbyshire
53 **Lost Lad,** Derwent Edge, Derbyshire
54 **Shiverpool Tours,** Liverpool
55 **Delph Tavern,** Wigan, Greater Manchester
56 **The Spinning Statue** at Manchester Museum
57 **All Saints Burial Ground,** Manchester
58 **Smithills Hall,** Bolton, Greater Manchester
59 **Haunted Haworth Ghost Walks,** Keighley, West Yorkshire
60 **The Bloody Tour of York,** North Yorkshire
61 **Clifford's Tower,** York, North Yorkshire
62 **Dick Turpin's Grave,** York, North Yorkshire
63 **The York Ghost Merchants,** North Yorkshire
64 **The York Dungeon,** North Yorkshire
65 **Treasurer's House,** York, North Yorkshire
66 **The Old Swan Hotel,** Harrogate, North Yorkshire
67 **Mother Shipton's Cave,** Knaresborough, North Yorkshire
68 **The Pendle Witches,** Roughlee, Lancashire
69 **The Woodplumpton Witch,** nr Preston, Lancashire
70 **Samlesbury Hall,** Preston, Lancashire
71 **The Blackpool Tower Dungeon,** Blackpool, Lancashire
72 **The Rock-Cut Graves,** Heysham, Lancashire
73 **Lancaster Castle,** Lancashire
74 **In Search of Dracula,** Whitby, North Yorkshire
75 **Whitby Goth Weekend,** North Yorkshire
76 **The Claife Crier,** Windermere, Cumbria
77 **The Lake District Corpse Roads,** Cumbria
78 **Castlerigg Stone Circle,** Keswick, Cumbria
79 **The Cursing Stone of Carlisle,** Cumbria
80 **The Poison Garden at Alnwick,** Northumberland
81 **Chillingham Castle,** Northumberland
82 **Bamburgh Castle,** Northumberland

48 Creswell Crags, Worksop, Nottinghamshire

See the largest collection of witch marks in the country

Turn the clocks back a few hundred years and you'll arrive in a land obsessed with witchcraft and superstition. The passing of the Witchcraft Act of 1563 made witchcraft or even associating with witches a crime punishable by death. Some people made a living out of hunting witches and bringing them to trial, often doing very nicely out of it. King James I (r. 1603–25, England and Ireland) was fascinated by it and wrote a defence of witch-hunting in his *Daemonologie* book of 1597. Many trials took place throughout the 17th century. Public hangings often attracted large crowds. And during these turbulent years when fear was often rife, worried folk came from far and wide to scratch marks in a cave they hoped would protect them and their loved ones.

Creswell Crags sits on the border between Nottinghamshire and Derbyshire. Visitors to this popular attraction will find a series of caves once famed for their cave art. During the last Ice Age, this was the most northerly inhabited place in Europe and some of those who took shelter in Creswell's caves etched scenes into the rocky walls. But in 2018, a chance discovery was made by two subterranean enthusiasts on one of the popular cave tours. On their way out of the visitor centre, they told the manager how much they liked the cave art ... and also the witch marks. This was the first time the Creswell Crags witch marks had been mentioned; certainly the staff here had no knowledge of them at that time. But, sure enough, an expert from Leicester University confirmed the authenticity of these strange markings. Not only that, but they also made it clear just how significant a find this was; although witch marks had been found in the UK before, this was the biggest collection of such superstitious writing by far. The number of marks in one cave alone reaches into the high hundreds. Witch marks have now been found in every one of the caves at Creswell Crags. It's thought they could have been made over a period of 300 years and so would have involved many people from the region.

But what are the markings and why were they scratched onto the walls of these ancient caves? Different symbols were written here, the most common being a 'VV' in reference to Mary, the Virgin of Virgins. You'll also find 'PM' for Pace Maria. Those travelling to the caves were probably terrified of something that had started to affect their lives and wanted to ward off evil spirits to keep their friends and families safe. This may have been crop failure, or could have been linked to serious diseases spreading through the population. Maybe people in their village were dying. Something, and perhaps we'll never know for sure, led them to make their own journey to Creswell Crags and etch the superstitious markings into the dark walls.

The location of these markings is also fascinating. In other places around the world, such scratched symbols have been made at the most accessible place, the easiest place to reach. But not here. Some of the 'VV' scratched markings are found in the far reaches of the cave, a fair way back and just before a passage descends into the bowels of the Earth. Did these worried folk think something lurked down there? Were they trying to keep the demons underground?

To see the witch marks and experience the fascinating caves for yourself, you must visit the website and book onto a tour. It's led by experienced and informative guides and is the only way to get access to these protected areas. The tours book up in advance because, as you can imagine, they are incredibly popular. But it's well worth it. Standing in the dark of the caves is an eerie experience, and seeing so many witch marks gives you the opportunity to put yourself in the shoes of those desperate enough to come here hundreds of years before you, seeking a way to stave off the darkness and keep hope alive.

OPPOSITE The witch marks at Creswell were pointed out by a visitor.
BELOW The marks date back to a time of superstition and fear.

CRAGS RD, CRESWELL, WORKSOP, S80 3LH
WWW.CRESWELL-CRAGS.ORG.UK

49 Lyceum Theatre, Sheffield, South Yorkshire

Famous for hosting pantomimes, musicals and comedies, there's also plenty of drama at the Lyceum when the audiences go home...

This Grade II listed building on Sheffield's Tudor Square is part of the biggest complex of theatres in the country outside the West End. Along with the two stages at the Crucible Theatre and the nearby Montgomery Theatre, this South Yorkshire cultural hub hosts touring productions from London, premieres its own shows, showcases a wide range of music and, of course, is under the world's gaze when the World Snooker Championship breaks every spring. However, thespians aren't the only ones craving the attention at the Lyceum; there are plenty of spooks wanting to steal the show. Thankfully, there are some excellent tour guides to take you around the darkened theatre once the audiences have left and the curtains are closed.

There's been a theatre on this site since 1879, so plenty of time for ghosts to call it home. It first opened under the name Grand Varieties, then in 1890 it became known as Stacey's Circus, before being changed to Stacey's Theatre. Three years later, the wooden building burned to the ground and was replaced by the City Theatre. The City Theatre was renamed The Lyceum for a short time before being rebuilt as the Lyceum we know today, which opened in 1897. Designed by renowned theatre architect W.G.R. Sprague, it's one of the best surviving examples of his work. But it's

BELOW The Sheffield Lyceum ghost tour is reyt good.

not all gone according to script. When film and television started to dominate the entertainment scene, the Lyceum closed its doors in 1969, briefly became a bingo hall, and then sat redundant. Thankfully, a massive restoration project saw it reopen in 1990 and it's been entertaining Sheffield audiences ever since. And providing a home to a spectre or two.

After-hours ghost tours run a couple of times a month, with paranormal enthusiasts Jake Ross and Nicky Crewe taking the helm. When the shows are on, they're working front of house, but when the audience heads home they're embarking on a trip around the darkened theatre, looking for some old, ghostly friends. They decided to put the tour together because so many of the staff here experienced unusual sights and sounds, and they wanted to share the stories with the people of Sheffield and beyond. The pair have had some unnerving experiences of their own in the Lyceum, but they've never felt unsafe. The ghosts may be dead, they say, but they're still their colleagues.

So who might you come across late at night in the Lyceum? Well, there's the 'Lavender Lady', a mysterious spirit with a scent of lavender who brings intense melancholy with her. She's also thought to have left a single rose in the leading male's dressing room from time to time. A strong, commanding voice heard near the stage door is thought to belong to a long-dead former stage manager. Even on the other side, this dedicated individual reminds staff to maintain dress codes and keep noise down. But perhaps the most chilling tale is of the children that have been seen and heard in dressing room five. Even when there are no children in the building, these unexplained experiences have startled staff working in the quiet theatre. There is also a common sense that the theatre workers are being watched...

Book in advance for these popular tours – and don't be too alarmed if you hear somebody shout 'he's behind you!'.

NORFOLK ST, SHEFFIELD, S1 1DA
WWW.SHEFFIELDTHEATRES.CO.UK

50 Eyam, Derbyshire

Take a spine-tingling walk around this 'plague village', where the community sacrificed themselves to save the wider population

The beautiful village of Eyam in the Peak District National Park is quaint and surrounded by incredible limestone countryside. But while it may be a lovely place to live now, it harbours a horrific history of self-sacrifice during a time when the population was being ravaged by disease. Effectively sentencing many of their own to death, the villagers went into a 17th-century lockdown to save other communities in surrounding villages. Since then, ghostly sightings of victims have been spotted in and around these hills.

The bubonic plague arrived in Eyam during September 1665 when a parcel of flea-infested cloth was delivered from London to the village tailor, George

Viccars. He became the first person in the village to die of the terrible disease. Within days, others started falling ill and it became obvious the plague was spreading like wildfire. So the villagers made an extraordinary decision to isolate themselves to stop the spread. The lockdown went on for 14 months, and food deliveries were left by a rock outside the village, with payments of coins placed in vinegar to make sure they were clean.

The impact of the plague on Eyam was catastrophic. Of the 350 people living there, nearly 260 died and entire families were wiped out. The episode still defines the character of the village, with 'plague houses' displaying plaques to show who died where.

Regular ghost walks take place in the village; you'll need to book in advance to ensure you get a place. As well as learning a lot about the village's history, there's a chance you'll hear footsteps echoing

ABOVE We all fall down: the village saw more than half its population wiped out.

BELOW The village church houses information on the grisly events.

around the Miners Arms pub. Inside, guests have reported doors slamming and strange chuckling noises. But who are the ghosts? It's a mystery. In Eyam, so many people died during those fateful plague months and so many houses were affected, it's impossible to say.

In Eyam's churchyard the tragedy continues. The Riley Graves are where Elizabeth Hancock buried her husband and six children during the outbreak. It must have been an unimaginable, devastating time. Visitors to the site are often overwhelmed with sadness and some have claimed to have seen Elizabeth's semi-transparent ghost kneeling by the graves.

In the Plague Cottage where George Viccars lived and died, paranormal activity has also been reported. Shadowy figures have been seen. Footsteps have been heard. And in the surrounding countryside you can walk to the boundary stone, where goods were dropped off and coins were left in vinegar. You can see the hole in the rock where the money was left, and some say they have heard cries and voices from this location too.

The story of Eyam is one of a community's collective struggle and grief. It's an incredibly humbling tale which still has an emotional impact on visitors. The rumours of ghostly events only add to the intrigue of this tragic episode in history.

HAWKHILL ROAD, DERBYSHIRE, EYAM, S32 5QP
WWW.HAUNTINGNIGHTSGHOSTWALKS.CO.UK

51 Little John's Grave, St Michael's Church, Hathersage, Derbyshire

Take a trip to this idyllic Peak District village and you'll discover the grave of a literary giant – and possibly see the ghost of another

There are many reasons to visit Hathersage, one of the prettiest villages in the Peak District National Park. Enjoy a walk into the rocky hills, take a bike ride to nearby Bakewell or simply relax at one of the many lovely coffee shops. The more adventurous may want to bring their swimwear and go for a dip in the famous outdoor heated swimming pool. But for those interested in legends and spooky rumours, this picturesque place is home to one of the most famous – and largest – graves in the country.

The story of Robin Hood and his Merry Men has been passed down through generations, written up in countless books and made into some brilliant – and some terrible – films and TV shows. Both children and adults have a fondness for the story of the lovable outlaw who supposedly took valuables from the wealthy and distributed them among the poor. Just how much of it is true and whether it was actually that simple a case of wealth redistribution, we will never know. Did he wear a green cap and have an awesome aim with a bow and arrow? Did he take on the Sheriff of Nottingham? Was Robin Hood's Cave near Hathersage really one of his hangouts? Did he really have a fight on a log with a giant of a man known ironically as Little John and then become his good friend?

According to legend and a sizeable proportion of Hathersage's population, the latter claim is definitely true. It has to be. For when you head up the hill to the graveyard at St Michael and All Angels Church, you will find a sign directing you to his final resting place. The huge grave that lies in this atmospheric churchyard has been a focal point for folklore and the odd ghostly tale. Located in an idyllic Peak District setting and a short but tough climb up the hill, this sacred place is as much connected to the Robin Hood legend as the Major Oak in Sherwood Forest and Nottingham Castle.

Finding the grave is easy enough. It's beneath the big yew tree and there's a headstone announcing that Little John is buried here, referring to him as the 'friend and lieutenant of Robin Hood'. There's even a replica of his trademark wooden pole next to his grave. A panel there states how Little John died in a cottage to the east of the church, which has since been destroyed.

The first written evidence of Little John's existence can be traced back to an 18th-century story, but there was local talk about a huge man and the adventures he got into long before. Further evidence came in 1784 when a man called James Shuttleworth excavated the grave and discovered a

BELOW Hathersage church is at the centre of the Robin Hood legend.

RIGHT Not so little, John was a local giant.

femur that measured an incredible 76cm (30in) long. A femur this length indicates the person buried here would have been over 2.4m (8ft) tall! It certainly sounds like the frame of the man we imagine Little John to be. Shuttleworth was apparently plagued by misfortune after he exhumed the bone, troubles which continued until it was reburied.

Elsewhere in Hathersage, there are other strange and mysterious legends, including rumours of a 'White Lady' haunting the vicarage. Some even believe this to be the ghost of Charlotte Brontë, who spent at least three weeks staying in the vicarage when researching her novel *Jane Eyre* in the summer of 1845. Lovely Hathersage, then, is a place for historic, well-known and much-loved ghosts.

MAIN ROAD, HATHERSAGE, HOPE VALLEY, DERBYSHIRE, S32 1BB

52 Winnats Pass, Castleton, Derbyshire

Pull on your walking boots and set off on a haunted hike in the Peak District, passing the scene where two young lovers were tragically killed

Welcome to the glorious vistas of the Peak District! This is Britain's oldest National Park and, sandwiched as it is between Manchester and Sheffield, with good train and bus connections, it pulls in plenty of visitors.

Castleton is one of the most popular of Derbyshire's lovely villages. It can be rammed with day-trippers on a warm summer day, though visit midweek in winter and there'll not be many people about. Most people arrive here to admire the views, maybe take a hike and then retire to enjoy a drink in one of its pubs or cafés. What walkers in this quaint corner of the Peak District don't expect to hear while they're out and about are terrifying voices and screams in the wind. The visitor guides (apart from this one!) don't tend to mention that you could spot mysterious spectres and experience that awful feeling of being watched as you traipse over the limestone landscape. But the hills around Castleton house a dark secret – one of murder, tragedy, guilt and remorse.

Walk to the west of Castleton and you'll soon come to a magnificent show cave known as the Devil's Arse, itself famous for being a haunted location. Beyond that, Speedwell Cavern's underground boat journey to a former lead mine is always popular. Continue further and you'll reach Winnats Pass, a steep gorge cut through the white limestone, laden with the tiny fossils of sea creatures from when this part of the world lay beneath a tropical sea. The dramatic edges of the pass and its steep ascent make it a go-to challenge for walkers and cyclists. But when two lovers passed through this way in 1758 on their way to be married, things were far from pretty.

Their names were Alan and Clara, and they were running away to get hitched in the Peak Forest, one of the only places in England at the time where you didn't need to have parental consent to be married. As they passed through this narrow, winding gorge on their way to what they thought was a happy future, they came across five lead miners who took a menacing interest in their valuables.

Alan was beaten to death as the miners stole their possessions. Clara was dragged away from the scene and killed, with both bodies being buried in the wild landscape. After they were discovered years later, the pair were buried at the church in Castleton. Their spirits, though, are said to be restless up in the heights of the pass. Screams have been heard, shadowy figures seen. Some cyclists have even reported a sense of being pulled back as they ascend the pass, as if Alan and Clara are trying to warn them. I've cycled up there, though in my case the only thing pulling me back was my level of fitness.

As for the miners who committed the crime, they were never convicted but led troubled lives. One was killed falling from a cliff near the scene, another died after being hit by a rock. The third committed suicide, riddled with guilt, and the fourth developed severe mental health problems. The last one to survive confessed on his death bed 20 years after the event, unable to hold the terrible secret anymore.

WINNATS PASS, HOPE VALLEY, DERBYSHIRE, S33 8WA

BELOW The murders in the High Peak still haunt the village of Castleton.

53 Lost Lad, Derwent Edge, Derbyshire

Take a hike to an eerie Peak District hill, where tragedy struck and mysterious happenings have been reported

Accessible thanks to the many footpaths heading high up into the hills from Ladybower Reservoir and the A57 in Derbyshire, Derwent Edge is a magical place and home to some unusual place names. Salt Cellar, Cakes of Bread and Dove Stone all refer to the millstone grit tors that poke up from the peaty ridge on the horizon. Here and Dartmoor are the best-known areas in the country with both peat and tors. And, a little way further along, beyond Back Tor, you'll come across Lost Lad. While some of the other tors in the area were named after the unusual shape of the rocks that litter this landscape, Lost Lad derived its title from a terrible tragedy that occurred here one harsh winter.

Abraham Lowe was a 13-year-old shepherd boy from a farm in the village of Derwent, a place now submerged by water following the construction of Ladybower Reservoir. He set out with his dog to get the family's flock to safety before the weather turned, but was trapped in a horrendous blizzard and died of hypothermia. Searches took place for Abraham but it was months later, in the spring, before his body was discovered. He had died huddled together with his dog, who had loyally refused to leave his master's side. The grim discovery was made by another shepherd who had spotted some writing that had been scratched onto a rock near where Abraham was found. It simply said 'lost lad'.

The story understandably saddened the local population at the time and some paid their respects by establishing a cairn on the spot of the tragic event. Each time they came up the hill to remember Abraham, they added another small stone. That cairn is still there, and today this hill has taken on the name Lost Lad, as it now appears on OS maps of the area.

But our story does not end there. In the years following the sad death of the teenager, there have been several ghostly sightings on and around Lost Lad, particularly in the middle of winter and when snow has started to fall. Nearby farmers and hikers are among those to have reported seeing a boy and his dog around the cairn, with others hearing voices on the wind. One of the most famous sightings occurred in 1983 when a teacher from Manchester was walking along Derwent Edge. He was so convinced the boy and his dog were there that he called out to say hello. But he received no reply and the pair then vanished.

If you head up here in winter, especially on a weekday, you're unlikely to come across many people and there will be a very eerie atmosphere. Perhaps better, then, to save your visit for a warm day in the summer, when there will be plenty of hikers. You can then enjoy the toposcope installed at Lost Lad, a

OPPOSITE Snow had fallen and the lad was lost on this spot.

360-degree map identifying the many peaks visible on the horizon.

The spine-tingling stories don't end there. In nearby Edale, reports of a large black dog wandering the Peak District hills managed to put the chills into many local people. The large beast was reported to be killing sheep on local farms as far back as the 1920s. And in the 1950s, one young girl from the village spoke of seeing a big black dog and trying to stroke it – but her hand only touched the air. Adults have also reported seeing this mysterious beast. It seems there is plenty of paranormal funny business to keep enthusiasts occupied in our oldest and most highly treasured National Park.

PATHS LEAD TO LOST LAD FROM CUTTHROAT BRIDGE ON THE A57 AND FROM THE DERWENT VALLEY

54 Shiverpool Tours, Liverpool

Enjoy a magical mystery tour around the city's most spooky locations

Liverpool is one of the finest cities in the UK, with a rich culture of music (the Beatles being Liverpool's most famous export), football and comedy attracting thousands of visitors. The redevelopment of the city following the industrial decline of the 1970s and 1980s has been remarkable, making it a hot city-break destination. But the glitz of the modern bars, hotels and shops mask some darker episodes in the town's history. This was a city that suffered terribly during 19th-century cholera outbreaks, while it was deeply connected to the appalling Transatlantic Slave Trade and working practices during the Industrial Revolution meant many inhabitants experienced horrendous conditions. Although *Rubber Soul* may have stood the test of time, not all Liverpool souls have settled well, it seems.

Fortunately, there's a popular company that specialises in taking aspiring ghost hunters through the city's streets, and pausing to investigate some of the most chilling events in Merseyside history. And their name is the envy of many a ghost tour guide – Shiverpool! Head to the website to book your chilling tour, knowing it will be delivered by entertaining and talented, costumed storytellers with a love for lending the evening a theatrical

BELOW You'll discover the Shiverpool tour to be one of the most atmospheric there is.

twist. You could opt to learn about spooky cemeteries or the gruesome history of the 'auld town', but the most popular – and original – Liverpool ghost tour is the Hope Street Shivers.

Starting off from the Philharmonic Dining Rooms, one of the city's most famous and architecturally splendid pubs, there'll be tales of ghosts right from the off. Did you hear about the spectral waiter who continues to serve drinks in the pub long after his death? And the man in the cap who has been sighted alone, maybe just wanting some company to enjoy a posthumous pint?

Liverpool is unusual in that it has two cathedrals, both of which feature in the tour. The huge, Gothic Anglican Cathedral was completed in the 1970s but occupies the site of a centuries-old graveyard. Lurking beneath this massive structure are cholera pits from the 1830s and 1840s, where thousands of victims were laid to rest. Some can still be seen and heard, according to hunters of the paranormal.

The Cathedral Quarter is known for its Georgian Old Town, with some brilliantly designed and historically significant homes lining the streets. Not all is well within these houses, however. Tragic stories of murder, accidents, illness and unhappiness lurk beyond some of these doors – as do some melancholy spirits.

Elsewhere on the tour, you'll take in the mysterious pyramidal tomb of Will McKenzie, the most famous of the city's undead who is said to have bet his soul with the devil and now restlessly walks the local streets. And there's also a stop at the famous Wellington Rooms, now abandoned but once the scene of posh parties for the city's wealthy. It also opened as the Irish Centre, which might explain the Irish banshee that has appeared here a few times. It's an omen of imminent death, so make sure you've paid all your debts and have a clean pair of pants on before you set off.

TICKETS AVAILABLE ONLINE OR AT THE INFORMATION CENTRE AT 5 WALL ST, LIVERPOOL, L1 8JQ
WWW.SHIVERPOOL.CO.UK

55 Delph Tavern, Wigan, Lancashire

This 'paranormal hotpot' of a Lancashire pub is said to be home to several troubled northern souls

The Lancashire town of Wigan is best known for its pier, strong connection to Northern Soul music and its very own 'kebab' – a savoury meat pie sandwiched between a buttered barm cake (bread bap). But this corner of the country is also famous for having its fair share of spooks, with two haunted pubs and a historic hall forming a triangle of local hauntings. The 'Wigan Triangle' is a tasty prospect for paranormal enthusiasts who fancy downing a pint and trying the local delicacy during their visit.

Our journey begins in the village of Orrell at the Delph Tavern, just 45m (150ft) into Lancashire. This inconspicuous pub is in a normal enough

LEFT The Delph is one of the most haunted pubs in northern England.

residential area, but beyond its white walls you'll discover more than a few strange stories. The pub was built close to Dawber Delph, a dangerous disused quarry that has been the site of multiple fatalities over the years, and a few restless spirits seem to linger at this watering hole. One is a woman in Victorian dress, who loiters near the back of the pub, possibly the wife of a quarryman. More common occurrences include patrons experiencing mysterious cold spots, seeing glasses move on their own and even smash, and hearing footsteps in rooms that are empty. And wait – was that a shadowy figure moving across the bar?

The Delph Tavern was built in the 1700s and has been hosting patrons ever since. Some like it so much they've never left. One of the pub's spookiest happenings is even available for you to watch on social media (check out YouTube and TikTok) after it drew the attention of paranormal experts. Look closely at the CCTV footage and you'll see an orb of light moving by a brick wall in the bar area in the middle of the night. It's clearly visible, but at that time in the morning might have gone unnoticed, were it not for the security alarms being set off at exactly that time. When the landlord checked the bar, nobody was found, but he reviewed the footage and saw the cameras had picked up the mysterious light. Spooky, eh?

Another middle-of-the-night story involved a woman walking her dog past the pub at 4am and seeing a man drinking at the bar with a light on. When the woman checked with the landlord, he said nobody was there. But she's not the only one to see apparitions of drinkers at the Delph. In the 1960s, several people had a vision of a drinker who, when approached, simply disappeared.

Patrons of a nearby pub, the Mount, have also experienced a number of unexplained events, including cold spots, mysterious shadows and pints moving along the table. Put the two together and it could make for a haunted pub crawl, including several spirits of both types!

And while you're in the Wigan area, check out Haigh Hall. Apparitions of children have been spotted here, playing on the staircase and in the gardens. Childish laughter has been heard in the grounds. The basement has proved to be a particular focus of paranormal teams with specialist recording equipment; they've captured voices thought to be those of servants from decades ago. Stories of furniture and equipment moving have also emanated from the hall. The 'Wigan Triangle' is certainly not for the faint of heart…

TONTINE RD, ORRELL, WIGAN, WN5 8UJ

56 The Spinning Statue at Manchester Museum

Witness the famous Ancient Egyptian figure that mysteriously rotates in a glass cabinet

Artefacts removed from Ancient Egypt are famed for reportedly having brutal and complex curses placed upon them. Such cursed objects have provided the inspiration for many books and films, some of which, admittedly, are wildly exaggerated. But warnings written on tombs were designed simultaneously to deter grave robbers and protect the dead in the afterlife, and clearly not everybody paid attention to them: several expedition members met with untimely and suspicious deaths after a raid on Tutankhamun's tomb. The 'Curse of the Pharaohs', then, was not something to be taken lightly...

Amid this supernatural backdrop, the eyes of the world's media turned to the Manchester Museum in 2013 when it

BELOW Step inside the museum to see an exhibit shrouded in mystery.

appeared an ancient statue from Egypt was, er, moving on its own. It sounds spooky, even impossible. But it was true. Staff spotted it first, but cameras later captured it on film; the 25cm (10in) tall figure of a man – thought to date to 1800 BC – was indeed rotating slowly inside its glass cabinet, without any outside interference. It was there for all to witness. Could we be looking at a cursed artefact trying to communicate with museumgoers, or is there a more scientific explanation for the spinning exhibit?

The 4,000-year-old statuette depicts Neb-Sanu standing with his arms crossed over his chest. Discovered in a tomb and made of serpentine stone, it is likely a representation of the deceased and designed to help this individual pass safely into the afterlife.

The Manchester Museum acquired the statue with lots of other Egyptian artefacts in the early 20th century; it had sat on display quite happily for many years before its twisting antics were discovered. And the plot was to thicken. Neb-Sanu's statue always moved in the same direction, gently rotating anticlockwise. What's weirder, the statue only moved during the day and remained still at night. It was like the movie *Night at the Museum*, but in reverse.

Soon academics, including the physicist Professor Brian Cox, began weighing in, as they tend to do, to try and find a scientific explanation for the phenomenon. They started to pick up good vibrations, giving the scientific community excitations. Buses, cars, people walking – these all contributed to the tiny vibrations picked up in the room. These vibrations, it's thought, were helping to slowly move the statue, a process accentuated by the uneven weight distribution it carried and an uneven base.

The debate went viral on social media and curious news crews added to the speculation. Visitor numbers shot up at the museum, with supernatural fans intrigued by the statue and hoping to see evidence of it moving for themselves. Could it be linked to a curse on Neb-Sanu? Did it indicate his soul was restless in the afterlife? Was he trying to get a message back to us, sending a warning perhaps? All these theories did the rounds, despite everyone knowing the boffins with the white coats were probably right about the vibration idea. But still, looking at the small statue in the glass cabinet and knowing the rumours of other Egyptian supernatural tales, it's hard not to imagine you're part of a bigger story that began on the banks of the River Nile some 4,000 years ago.

OXFORD RD, MANCHESTER, M13 9PL
WWW.MUSEUM.MANCHESTER.AC.UK

RIGHT You spin me right round: Neb Sanu.

57 All Saints Burial Ground, Manchester

Take a moment to relax and reflect in a city square that once had a more macabre use

On a sunny day in the north of England, students from Manchester Metropolitan University can be found hanging out on the grass in All Saints Park. Some will be relaxing between lectures in the nearby uni buildings. Others may head to the grassy square to enjoy lunch or grab a coffee with friends. Reading a book, listening to music, recovering from a night out; this is a very popular place to spend downtime in the middle of the urban jungle that is Manchester. Black railings surround the lovely park, with gated entrances on every side. The hustle and bustle of city life continues beyond those railings, but within, there's a chance to catch your breath. But most of the park's visitors will be blissfully unaware of the dark secret lurking beneath them, their Jane Austen books and their flat whites.

This place has been dedicated to R&R since the 1930s, when a change of use turned the city centre square into a children's play area. It took 25 years of negotiations to see the park come into existence, but it was described as being one of the brightest places in Manchester when it opened in May 1935. People flocked here from all over Greater Manchester, and during the first six weeks of opening, some 30,000 kids came here to play. It must have buzzed with fun, noise and excitement. And maybe a lollipop or two.

ABOVE The square is a peaceful place with a fascinating history.

But below the surface of the lush grass in All Saints Park, a scary secret looms. For this was once a burial ground for Manchester's poorest residents, and a burial ground on an enormous scale. All Saints Church stood on the site until it was heavily damaged during the Blitz, and its burial ground was for local parishioners. The first to be interred here was 21-year-old Fanny Knowles. She lived on London Road and was buried here in 1820. That year, another 54 people were buried. But the numbers soon started to increase. By the 1850s, there were more than ten people a week being buried, and over 600 dead bodies were laid to rest here in 1851.

The numbers were becoming unsustainable. Below the surface of this lovely Manchester hideaway there are thought to be as many as 16,000 bodies, crammed into a relatively tiny space during the course of the 19th century. By the turn of the next century, this burial ground had seen better days. Some of the graves were starting to sink and flooding caused considerable damage, along with decades of exposure to the wind and rain. Something needed to be done, but during the transition to it becoming a park, the decision was made not to move the remains of the dead. So they're all still down there, thousands of corpses a few short feet beneath the students catching up over a cappuccino.

This is still consecrated ground, so even though it's been a children's park and an open, grassy space, people are asked to be extremely respectful when they visit. The only clue about the square's history as a former burial ground is a small marker with a plaque. It points out the role of the university in improving the square for public use, but urges visitors to show respect worthy of such a place and refrain from playing ball games and dropping litter. Seems fair.

GROSVENOR SQUARE, MANCHESTER, M15 6BH

58 Smithills Hall, Bolton, Greater Manchester

Dare you enter this medieval hall believed to be haunted by several spirits?

Look, if you build a large family home on top of a medieval cemetery, you're asking for trouble. Anybody who's watched the 1982 fantasy-horror *Poltergeist* knows this. But that appears to be what happened when Smithills Hall was constructed, a fabulous building with a formidable history – and a place where ghosts are thought to hang out in droves.

After the First World War, like many large country homes, the costs and taxes were too much to deal with, and Smithills was bought by Bolton Council. It became a residential home and later a day care centre before being restored and opened to the public.

There's particular interest in the Withdrawing Room of this Grade I listed building. It was here in the 1950s that human bones were discovered beneath the floor, this being one of the most troubling stories during the ghost-hunt evening events that are held here. Some of you may not be brave enough to read on, let alone book in and head to this creepy room in the middle of the night.

Smithills Hall still retains many of its original features from when it was built in 1335. It's spent nearly 700 years as a family home and had various sections added on as the centuries rolled by. With this amount of history linked to the site, no wonder this is one of England's most haunted houses. There's practically a spook in every room. Let's take the Green Room, for example. In 1555, Bolton farmer George Marsh was brought here to face the estate owner, Robert Barton, on the charge of being a Protestant. Not a good look during the reign of devoted Catholic Queen Mary. Marsh was burned at the stake. But one family of visitors pointed to a man up in the Green Room when they were being shown out at the end of the day. The member of staff said the visitors were the last family and locked the door behind them. So was that the spirit of George Marsh loitering inside?

ABOVE AND BELOW Smithills Hall: home to much paranormal mystery.

There have also been strange happenings in the chapel. A volunteer working at the hall before it was open in the morning went into the chapel and saw somebody on their knees, praying. When he went to fetch a colleague and returned, the worshipping figure had vanished. Another member of staff removing dead flowers from the chapel was pushed from behind into a wall by a force that left them with minor injuries. And when this was a residential home, some staff heard horses' hooves galloping in the grounds. Spooky.

Talk of such paranormal events has echoed round this hall for many a year,

and there have been plenty of ghost hunts carried out here to try and get to the bottom of what's going on.

During investigations led by professional ghost hunters Haunted Happenings, there have been apparitions of a priest that have turned the event into a terrifying experience. Combined with the many small, dark rooms and spooky corridors, an investigation of this particular building is said to be only for the very brave. If you're one of those brave souls who can stick out a nighttime ghost investigation, you can book onto one of the evenings at www.hauntedhappenings.co.uk. And if you do sign up for the event, it will be an evening you won't forget in a hurry. This is not a ghost tour given by a retired history teacher in cosplay. You'll be handling proper ghost-hunting equipment, such as EMF meters, and using older methods like glass divination and Ouija boards. There's also an opportunity to hold vigils here, and some people even want to take themselves off on their own. Frightening stuff, but the hall does get returning visitors, seeking an intense thrill all over again.

SMITHILLS DEAN RD, BOLTON, BL1 7NP
WWW.BOLTONLAMS.CO.UK

59 Haunted Haworth Ghost Walks, Keighley, West Yorkshire

Learn about spooky happenings in the village where the Brontë sisters wrote their famous works

Surrounded by windswept moors inspiring a whole swathe of 19th-century novels, this lovely East Yorkshire village still seems as though from another time. The stage is magnificently set in Haworth for some atmospheric, chilling storytelling as the sky darkens, the streets empty of day-trippers and the old street lamps provide an eerie backdrop for supernatural stories. Embarking on the Haunted Haworth Ghost Walk is a must-do activity here.

Haworth is a popular destination for literary fans from around the world, drawn to step inside the Brontë Parsonage, where some of England's most celebrated novels were penned. But be warned – some visitors have reported experiencing cold spots and the feeling of being watched inside the famous sisters' old home. The parsonage is thought to be the most haunted building in the village, with some claiming Emily Brontë's ghost walks the halls. Activity has also been reported around Branwell, the less talked about Brontë brother, who fell to alcoholism and tuberculosis.

At night, some have even heard the melancholic cries of a woman, leaving them unable to explain exactly where it is coming from in the village. One source of this tragic sound has been the car park behind the Black Bull pub. Way back in the 19th century, beer was brewed here using water from an old well, which was located where the car park now lies. The water in the well had filtered down

ABOVE Haunted Haworth has plenty of spooky tales up its sleeve.

through the graveyard next to the pub.

Another mysterious weeping lady wandering the streets of Haworth was actually known to the Brontë sisters. Elizabeth Gaskell wrote about the spirit in her biography *The Life of Charlotte Brontë*, which was published in 1857 and explains how the author of *Jane Eyre* had heard tales of an unhappy mother and daughter remaining in Haworth long after their death.

Out on the moors, you can go wandering up to Top Withens, an old, ruined farm house thought to be the windswept inspiration for *Wuthering Heights*. Long regarded as haunted, hikers recall hearing voices on the wind. But most chilling of all is the sound of a galloping horse making its way along these rural tracks. Read the novels and poems of the Brontë sisters before you go. Maybe listen to some of Emily Brontë's haunting poems set to music by the Unthanks. All this will add a good deal to your day out exploring haunted Haworth.

But now back to the Black Bull, where you might want to go and enjoy a pint after you've finished your walk. Several unexplained events have reportedly occurred here, particularly around the fireplace where Branwell Brontë liked to sit and drink. Will you be one of the people who feels uneasy in this spot? Will you hear the sound of him coughing? Will you witness glasses moving?

Tourists return to Haworth year after year, drawn in by the way the village is almost frozen in time. Many, I'm sure, would also confirm this West Yorkshire gem has a mysterious feeling, especially in winter months when there is a cold mist in the air. To get the most out of your visit, join knowledgeable and entertaining storyteller Adam, who runs regular ghost walks throughout the year, which can be booked on his Haunted Haworth website.

BOOK IN ADVANCE AND MEET ON MAIN ST, HAWORTH, KEIGHLEY, BD22 8DA
WWW.HAUNTEDHAWORTH.CO.UK

60 The Bloody Tour of York, North Yorkshire

Let 'Mad Alice' lead you through the city's ghost lore on an unforgettable evening of spooky stories

Fully immersed in character and with an impressive wardrobe straight out of yesteryear, your guide for this much-loved York ghost tour assumes the role of troubled local character 'Mad Alice' Smith. York is a city boasting more than its fair share of ghostly goings-on, with some stories dating back to the days Romans called this place home, or '*domus*' I guess. Because it's got gruesome tales of murder and terror oozing from every street corner, there are a few ghost tours to choose from in York. Be assured – 'Mad Alice' delivers one of the best.

The setting for this spooky stroll couldn't be more perfect. York city centre's higgledy-piggledy streets, atmospheric lighting and centuries-old buildings at times appear like a chilling film set. Church bells chime around the city on the hour and the imposing York Minster provides a fabulous backdrop, as timeless as it is memorable. The terrible tales you'll hear about on the tour certainly match the surroundings. The very worst of the city's 2,000-year history comes together in gory detail.

Perhaps the city's most infamous son is Guy Fawkes – born in York and

BELOW Go down a paranormal rabbit hole with Mad Alice.

RIGHT The world-famous Shambles in York is the heart of many a ghost walk.

embarking on a path that almost led to the destruction of Parliament in 1605 rather than his own demise. Highwayman Dick Turpin also has strong connections to York, though he wouldn't be happy with all of them. He stole plenty of riches in the region but was also hanged here in 1739. And in the 1580s, this patch was home to Margaret Clitherow, who was sentenced to death for harbouring a Catholic priest at a time when they were being persecuted. She didn't plead guilty and remained silent during her trial, which meant her execution was the most horrific to be performed at the time. Clitherow was executed by pressing – large weights placed on her body gradually crushed her to death. And to think York looks such a pleasant place today!

But just who was 'Mad Alice'? Many of the details are a little patchy, lost down the decades. But we do know she was called Alice Smith and she lived on what is now Lund's Court, though at the time it was referred to as Mad Alice Lane. Tragically, the nickname she was given by townsfolk is likely to be down to her mental health problems, misunderstood at the time and prompting locals to label her as 'mad'. Her story is in some way an acknowledgement of the injustices suffered by those who had mental health issues in the past. Appallingly, historians believe Alice was jailed for her insanity and either died while incarcerated or was maybe even executed on the inside. There have been reported sightings of 'Mad Alice' in and around the area where she used to live, some unsuspecting passers-by noticing a shadowy figure moving in the alleyways and others feeling a sudden chill come across them. Book onto this tour and the odds are the only Mad Alice you'll see is the tour guide version – but I guess you never know. Either way, you're in for an unforgettable evening of rich, often harrowing, local history, told in a truly engaging and entertaining way.

BOOK ONLINE AND MEET AT
COLLEGE ST, YORK, YO1 7JF
WWW.THEBLOODYTOUROFYORK.CO.UK

61 Clifford's Tower, York, North Yorkshire

Step inside the scene of horrific antisemitic violence which still haunts this great northern city

Clifford's Tower is one of the most recognisable of York's many iconic buildings. It's also where one of the most horrific scenes in the city's violent history took place. The mound was initially built as a motte and bailey castle by William the Conqueror following his successful invasion of England in 1066. The tower was burned down by Danish invaders in 1069, an uprising which prompted a devastating response from the king as he laid waste to much of northern England. This wave of destruction became known as the Harrying of the North; some claim it laid the foundations for the north–south divide which continues to this day.

The most well known – and most traumatic – events that unfolded at the rebuilt tower in the centre of York took place in 1190, when members of the Jewish community came here seeking sanctuary on one terrifying night in March. Religious prejudice had been overflowing in England, resulting in attacks on Jewish people in several locations. In York, a mob started targeting the Jewish community and caused them to flee for their lives. They made their way to the tower, where they hoped they would be safe.

BELOW Clifford's Tower is one of York's most recognisable landmarks.

But none of the 150 people taking shelter in Clifford's Tower would survive the night. Fearing what would happen to them if they fell into the hands of the baying mob outside, many decided to take their own lives. In horrific scenes driven by fear, parents killed their own children and then killed each other. Others set fire to the keep in a bid to end it all before capture. Those that did survive this tragic affair were promised safe passage and lured out of the tower, only to be struck down as soon as they made it outside.

The tragic events that took place at Clifford's Tower have been linked to many chilling, paranormal stories down the ages. One of the most common tales associated with the site is the appearance of mysterious lights within the tower, described by some as being like flickering flames. Others claim to have seen shadowy figures lingering around the tower and heard disembodied cries. Are these somehow the timeless imprint of the terrified victims trapped in the tower all those centuries ago? Ghostly children have also been spotted near to the site, many of these strange happenings occurring at the same time as a sudden drop in temperature and feelings of intense sadness.

Today, Clifford's Tower is cared for by English Heritage and there has been significant investment in the visitor experience over recent years. It's one of the many must-do attractions York has to offer. But when you learn about the massacre of 1190, see artworks depicting it and stand on the spot where the terrible events took place, your visit becomes a melancholy, thought-provoking experience. Visitors are subdued as they try to imagine the events of that horrendous night. Ghostly stories may have been passed down the generations, but this chapter of history is most chilling because it informs us about the dangers of a society that is intolerant of other cultures.

TOWER ST, YORK, YO1 9SA
WWW.ENGLISH-HERITAGE.ORG.UK/VISIT/PLACES/CLIFFORDS-TOWER-YORK

62 Dick Turpin's Grave, York, North Yorkshire

Legendary highwayman Dick Turpin moved to York before being captured and executed, with some saying his spirit still hangs out by his grave

Think of an 18th-century highwayman, donning a black hat and riding on a sturdy steed, and your mind is likely to jump straight to Dick Turpin. He's been depicted many times in paintings, films and novels, and his ghost is said to wander the streets of York where he was hanged. But although now synonymous with this northern city, Turpin embarked on his criminal career in London and Essex, carrying out various crimes and becoming a notorious outlaw with a price on his head. Too well known in the south and with the authorities closing in, he moved north and wound up in York under the name John Palmer. Despite having a new name, this did not mean Turpin had turned over a new leaf; his crime spree continued unabated, and he was accused of stealing both sheep and horses, the latter being a crime punishable by death. After flinging him in prison, the authorities were still not aware they had caught the mighty Dick Turpin, but that all changed when he wrote a letter to his brother-in-law. Incredibly, his handwriting was recognised by somebody working at the post office and the outlaw was identified. Unlucky, Dick. He was sentenced to death and remained pretty defiant to the end, bowing to crowds who had come out to witness his death.

Turpin holds an unusual place in British folklore. His crimes were violent, affected many people in many communities, and invoked terror among law-abiding folk. And yet he is often depicted as a heroic figure, dashing and daring and at times confused by some with lovable rogue Robin Hood. York has certainly embraced the legend of Dick Turpin and it helps with the tourist industry. His grave in St George's Churchyard is the only one still in an upright position, the rest lying flat on the ground. It often has flowers laid by it. Visitors go to pay their respects and ghost tours regular include it as one of their stops. There have been many ghostly sightings at the grave and on the surrounding streets of a mysterious figure in dress from Turpin's period, with many suggesting they have felt an unusual level of energy. And those horse hooves that have been heard ... could they be the ghost of Turpin's horse, Black Bess?

Some say Turpin's ghost wanders between the churchyard and Knavesmire, where he was hanged. As to why his spirit may be restless, well, apart from all the robbing and being executed, it's thought his body was almost stolen just after being buried. At that time, fresh corpses could raise a lot of money if given to the right medical practitioners wanting to carry out experiments on humans. Records show an attempt was made to move Turpin from his final resting place, but lime was added to his coffin to make his body unusable and deter the body snatchers from returning. Some reckon Turpin doesn't lie in this spot at all, that his body rests elsewhere and the stone was put up to pull in the visitors. But surely, the ghost in the hat and the galloping horse ain't gonna lie...

LEAD MILL LN, YORK, YO1 9QH

LEFT Stand and deliver: the final resting place of the most famous highwayman.

63 The York Ghost Merchants, North Yorkshire

Discover an atmospheric shop in the centre of spooky York selling handcrafted ghosts for you to look after

With its historic cobbled streets, quirky old buildings and more than its fair share of haunted pubs, York is well and truly on the ghost-hunter's map. And for many visitors to this haunting northern city, buying their own spectre and taking it home as a souvenir is now an essential part of the trip.

Walk down the particularly atmospheric Shambles, with its host of shops relating to magic and wizardry, and you'll come across York's own unique Ghost Merchants. That's right, a shop dedicated to the art of making and selling little ceramic spectres. You'll know which shop is the Ghost Merchants alright; there's always a sizable queue outside. The collectable phenomenon of York's

ABOVE Which unique spook will you take home for your shelf?

ghosts has become so huge that visitors from all over the world will line up along the Shambles and think nothing of waiting 30 minutes or more to get inside and choose their own, unique spirit.

After opening in 2019, the popularity of the little York ghosts skyrocketed and doesn't appear to be fading. It's easy to see why; the individual ghost that you choose to take home has the same shape as all the others, taking on the appearance of somebody with a bedsheet draped over their head for Halloween. But every ghost is one of a kind, handmade and painted with a unique design. These tiny ghosts have a creepy individuality, whether they're bought as mementos for a loved one or a good luck charm to sit on your own shelf. There's a black and green one on mine.

The social media team at the York Ghost Merchants has helped to create an electrifying buzz around the product. The website points out the shop is a member of the Sorrowful Guild of Master Ghost Merchants, and the only one currently in business. York ghosts have travelled to all corners of the world, wrapped in a spooky historical map of the city.

Part of the otherworldly charm of coming here is the experience itself. That includes waiting for your turn in the queue on this 14th-century street, while mystified passers-by query what you're waiting for and the costumed staff organise those heading in and out. Stepping inside the shop is like entering a different world. Dim lighting, wooden shelving, a hushed atmosphere; it all generates the feeling of a haunted Victorian study. The little ghosts are all around you, divided up into different issues and colours, with some being limited edition and others being more common. Ask the assistants to help you and you'll soon learn the differences between the designs. The hardest part of the experience will be deciding which one is right for you.

Part of the appeal of the York Ghost Merchants is the exclusivity. Every one of the ceramic ghosts is made in York, and they are all sold right here (availability on the shop's website is sporadic at best). To be certain of getting your own little ghost to haunt your home, you will just have to make the trip to York and wait patiently.

SHAMBLES, YORK, YO1 7LZ
WWW.YORKGHOSTMERCHANTS.COM

BELOW Some of the ghosts available to take away.
OPPOSITE York is a city with hauntings and spooky tales at every corner.

64 The York Dungeon, North Yorkshire

Enter a theatrical world where history comes to life and you can get up close to some famously scary Yorkshire folk

This is an experience that will entertain and educate, as well as bombard the senses in a session full of fun. A cast of actors and a host of special effects brings Yorkshire history to life as you enter different stages for some great little shows and interactive scenes. Expect jump scares, water sprays and a few very pungent smells. And with the help of a team dedicated to making you squirm and smile, you'll get to the know all about the darkest parts of York's history. In the last 2,000 years, York has had close encounters with Romans and Vikings, not to mention individuals like Isabella Billington, Guy Fawkes and Dick Turpin. Some would say this is a city which attracts trouble.

One of the bloodiest times in York's history came at the hands of the Vikings, and in the care of an axe-wielding warrior you'll learn more about daily life in the place they called Jorvik. If you're not of Viking descent, maybe don't shout about it, because the warrior is on the lookout for more slaves and these Vikings are not exactly renowned for their nice behaviour; you'll surely shudder when you discover how they performed the infamous 'blood eagle' on their enemies.

Leaving the Vikings behind, you come more up

LEFT The York Dungeon brings history to life in a thrilling way.

to date when you enter a house in York. But all is not well at 35 Stonegate. This is thought to be one of the most haunted homes in the city – and York is a city with a huge reputation for hauntings. You'll meet the housekeeper of the property and realise she's very scared of something. Listen carefully to her ghostly tale, but keep your wits about you. There's often somebody else in this room. Watching. And not all that welcoming...

One of the most notorious of York's sons is Guy Fawkes, who plotted to blow up Parliament on 5 November 1605. Born in the city in 1570, he'll tell you in person what his life was like in York and how he got involved as a conspirator against the authorities. You'll certainly remember, remember all the grim details about how he was caught and tortured for ten long days.

One of the best scenes is saved for last as you clamber into a carriage and begin a bumpy journey through time to an era when highwaymen were after your valuables – and often took them. Enter the stage coach driver, who shares grim tales about the things he's had to endure while trying to keep passengers safe. But this one's all about Dick Turpin, how he organised his reign of terror and tortured his victims – particularly if you didn't do exactly as he wanted. He paid the price, of course – the punishments for highway robbery were extremely severe.

The York Dungeon, like its sister attractions, is great at what it does. It makes gruesome parts of history fun through interactive, theatrical magic. And you'll leave with an insight into York's history that can't be gained anywhere else.

CLIFFORD ST, YORK, YO1 9RD
WWW.THEDUNGEONS.COM/YORK

65 Treasurer's House, York, North Yorkshire

The finances of York Minster were once overseen in this historic house, which has seen its fair share of spine-tingling events

Treasurer's House in the centre of York is a beautiful building that stands close to the phenomenally impressive York Minster. The house gets it name from its connection to the minster, because all of its finances were once controlled from here. But when Henry VIII took control of the Church of England in 1534 with the Act of Supremacy, the minster's treasurer was no longer needed and the building became property of the Crown. It was rebuilt in the 17th century to take on its present appearance, and bought by wealthy industrialist Frank Green in the 19th century. Funnily enough, when he gave it to the National Trust he promised he would come back and haunt them if anything happened that he was unhappy about. The National Trust has taken good care of the building, but staff apparently mention the sudden, wispy aroma of cigar smoke and suggest it could be Mr Green coming back to check up on his former home.

The most famous haunting of York's Treasurer's House is of Roman soldiers in full uniform marching through the cellar. Sounds unbelievable, doesn't it? And to be fair, it hasn't been reported that often, but there was a very famous case here in 1953 when a young plumber had the fright of his life. While 18-year-old apprentice Harry Martindale was mending pipes, he told of one Roman soldier walking

ABOVE The Treasurer's House.
BELOW A ghostly recreation of what was seen inside.

through the cellar, followed by a horse and – wait for it – another 20 Roman soldiers, walking two abreast. You can't make this stuff up. And all the centurions in question were missing the bottom part of their legs. It turns out the original Roman road sat around a foot lower than the cellar floor, so they were walking at the ground level they knew. Spooky.

Now, so many historic buildings make mention of a 'Grey Lady' (some of which we've covered in this book) that when you hear of another one it's tempting to shrug it off. But perhaps the prevalence of these ghosts with their faded appearance is evidence of their authenticity. Either way, there's a Grey Lady that's been sighted several times at the Treasurer's House in York. The action for this particular spectre seems to take place mostly in the Tapestry Room. Here you'll find an old mirror and it's said that if you stare into it for long enough, you'll see the Grey Lady appear in it.

Even more strange are the tales children have told when they broke past the security barrier and ran over to sit on one of the chairs. This has happened at least on a couple of occasions, and when the mortified parents ask their child why they did it the answer is startling. The youngsters said they were beckoned across the room to sit on the knee of the old lady. That would be the Grey Lady, I presume.

There's a café in the basement, which is a great place to take stock of your time spent here. Keep an eye out for the black cat – many customers have reported cuddling up to it. Try to keep calm if you do see it, for there is no cat living in the Treasurer's House. It is but another of the otherworldly legends that inhabits this place.

MINSTER YARD, YORK, YO1 7JL
WWW.NATIONALTRUST.ORG.UK/VISIT/YORKSHIRE/TREASURERS-HOUSE-YORK

66 The Old Swan Hotel, Harrogate, North Yorkshire

Stay in the hotel at the heart of Agatha Christie's greatest mystery

Internationally recognised as one of the greatest mystery writers of all time, Agatha Christie created much-loved detectives Hercule Poirot and Miss Marple. She wrote best-selling classic novels like *Murder on the Orient Express* and *Death on the Nile*, as well as being behind *The Mousetrap*, which is still the longest-running stage play in history. She is undoubtedly Queen of the Whodunnit. But perhaps the most mysterious story of all – and one considered by many to be unsolved – had Agatha Christie herself as the main protagonist. On 3 December 1926, she simply disappeared. Her car was discovered by a quarry near Guildford with some possessions inside, but she was nowhere to be found. Speculation mounted, media coverage magnified and the public became enthralled by what had happened to the famous crime writer. It was a real-life mystery, and it was 11 days before Agatha Christie was found. After a comprehensive search, she was discovered here in North Yorkshire, at a large hotel in Harrogate, now called the Old Swan. Little did she know, but she'd been recognised at the hotel by a musician who had then told the police. And so, one evening, Christie came down in the lift to dinner and found her husband and a police officer waiting for her. Awkward.

So, whodunnit? Christie seemed to have suffered some serious memory loss and claimed not to recognise her husband. Some say she took off wandering due to a psychiatric condition, others that she had a breakdown, while the more cynical reckon it was all a publicity stunt. She actually got a lot of hassle from the press for the incident, despite explaining to the *Daily Mail* in an interview that her 'disappearance' had been due to mental health issues, something not widely understood at the time.

With such strange occurrences in the 1920s, and the hotel now being forever associated with mysteries, there is a real intrigue about this North Yorkshire location. Mysterious shadows have been reported in the corridors and footsteps have been heard when nobody is about. Objects moving on their own, flickering lights, cold spots and claims of apparitions have all been reported here.

The ghost of Agatha Christie, who died in 1976, clearly haunts the Old Swan Hotel, even if only metaphorically. People come here to engage with this unexplained piece of history. You can stay in the room where she stayed, and every summer there is a crime writing festival where sleuths from all over get together to compare notes in a fittingly chilling setting.

And if you fancy solving a spooky challenge of your own, check out the hotel website for the next murder mystery night. These well-run, regular events have different themes and invite you to get into role to solve a crime. They're organised by a specialist group, include plenty of laughs and usually sell out. As well as booking the mystery dinner, you can also stay over on a weekend break. But will you have the stomach to stay in Agatha Christie's room?

SWAN RD, HARROGATE, HG1 2SR
WWW.CLASSICLODGES.CO.UK/THE-OLD-SWAN

BELOW Agatha was in this hotel all along.

67 Mother Shipton's Cave, Knaresborough, North Yorkshire

Venture into the space where the world-famous soothsayer lived with her Petrifying Well

ABOVE Mother knows best, and this one predicted all kinds of future events.

This is the tale of a woman cast out with her young child, forced to live in a cave and experiencing a life immersed in speculation of witchcraft and premonitions. Yet this famous North Yorkshire legend didn't end in a hanging or a witch hunt; rather it created one of the oldest tourist attractions in the country and even drew the attention of the king at the time. Visitors headed to Old Mother Shipton's Cave as long ago as the 17th century to see where the old woman who predicted the future used to live. And they marvelled at the Petrifying Well, which was located so close to her dwelling. Was it a coincidence that things turned to stone near her cave home? And just who was Old Mother Shipton?

Our story begins in 1488, when 15-year-old Agatha Southeil gave birth to a daughter. The baby was sadly born with birth defects and when Agatha refused to give the father's name, she and baby Ursula were banished to live in a cave, close to Knaresborough Castle. A couple of years later, the Abbot of Beverley took pity on the pair, taking in Ursula and sending Agatha to a convent. The mother and daughter never saw each other again. But the sadness doesn't end there. Ursula had a troubled childhood and was subjected to much taunting due to her looks. But as an adult, she married a carpenter from York called Tobias Shipton. When he died, she kept his name and moved herself back to the cave, after which she was given the title 'Old Mother' Shipton as she grew older.

While she lived in the Knaresborough cave, word soon spread about her humble and strange existence, and she became famous for predicting the future. She predicted the coming of the plague in 1665, quickly followed by the Great Fire of London in 1666. Some reckon Old Mother Shipton also predicted the defeat of the Spanish Armada. So renowned were her 'witchlike' predictions, she gained attention from King Henry VIII and messengers – reputedly including Cardinal Wolsey – were sent to liaise with her. The list of predictions that appear to have come true is lengthy, covering technical advancements like the invention of the aeroplane, iron ships and, it's been claimed, even the internet. Political events called by her include the French Revolution, American Civil War and the Reformation in England. Not surprising, then, that this Yorkshire troglodyte has been compared to that better-known predictor of events, Nostradamus.

The Petrifying Well is part of the cave site and was once thought to have supernatural properties linked to Mother Shipton because it literally turned items into stone. The geological explanation for this phenomena is found in the water, which has travelled through limestone and absorbed high levels of calcium carbonate. The minerals are left on objects in the cave, solidifying them over time. Today, many items have been placed inside the well, including children's toys and teddy bears. They look chilling after their stony transformation.

When you're in Knaresborough, keep an eye on the 'High Bridge' over the River Nidd. Old Mother Shipton, in one of her most famous prophecies, said the world would come to an end 'when this bridge is thrice fallen'. It has already collapsed once, in 1848, and was targeted by the Luftwaffe during the Second World War. Let's hope it holds steady a while longer...

PROPHECY HOUSE, HARROGATE RD, HIGH BRIDGE, KNARESBOROUGH, HG5 8DD
WWW.MOTHERSHIPTON.CO.UK

BELOW The Knaresborough bridge it is said will bring doom if it falls three times.

68 The Pendle Witches, Roughlee, Lancashire

Take a walk up to the top of this famous Lancashire hill, which will forever be associated with witchcraft and witch hunts

The Lancashire giant that is Pendle Hill rises to 557m (1,827ft) above sea level, a natural northern landmark that has an instantly recognisable outline. The summit is sometimes shrouded in mist, but this entire area is always shrouded in mystery and legend. It's a popular place to go hiking, but it is also the epicentre of witchcraft in Britain and the persecutions that followed. Ascending Pendle Hill and visiting the surrounding villages, then, offers both a spiritual and historical experience, an emotional opportunity to immerse yourself in the tales of the past and the stories of hauntings in the present day.

To this day, the area around Pendle Hill is synonymous with the Pendle Witch Trials of 1612, a dark episode in British history in which ten people were sentenced to death by hanging at nearby Lancaster Castle.

The people put on trial (only one of them was acquitted) were all from villages around this hill, a place of serious beauty but one possessing sinister undertones. The allegations against the accused were fuelled by superstition and paranoia. Much was down to the word of a nine-year-old girl called Jennet Device, her testimony resulting in her own mother, sister and brother being condemned to death.

There are many sinister stories associated with Pendle Hill, too many to be disregarded as mere hocus-pocus. The most talked about is the Ghost of

RIGHT Remembering Alice Nutter, the so-called 'witch' who lived in Roughlee.

Old Demdike. This is the spirit of Elizabeth Southerns, one of the local women accused of being a witch in the early 17th century. She's been known to appear on the hill itself, a cloaked figure walking with the stature of an old woman slowly moving across the countryside. It would be enough to fill any hiker on that distinctively domed hill with fear. Another ghost seen in the area belongs to Alizon Device, granddaughter of Old Demdike and one of the first to be accused. Some have said her figure reaches out to passers-by, almost crying out for help – yet no sound is made.

While Pendle Hill remains a remote place still visited today by modern witches and pagans, particularly during equinoxes and solstices, the surroundings can be equally spooky.

Some of the so-called witches lived in Newchurch-in-Pendle, where St Mary's Church is home to an 'eye of God' carved out of stone to ward off evil. You can see it just below the clock on the tower. Around Roughlee, where hanged 'witch' Alice Nutter used to live, a pale ghost has been spotted and unexplained energy forces felt by visitors. A statue of Alice stands as a reminder to the shocking witch hunts that took place here, which ripped communities apart and prematurely ended the lives of so many. Come here to take a walk and see where these infamous 'witches' once lived, but be prepared for an emotional time. Learning about these stories really brings home the human suffering that was felt during this dark period across rural Lancashire.

THE MOST COMMON PLACE TO START A WALK IS FROM BARLEY VILLAGE, BB12 9JX

69 The Woodplumpton Witch, nr Preston, Lancashire

Discover the grave of a woman thought to be a witch, now protected to stop her coming back from the dead

The atmospheric churchyard in the Lancashire village of Woodplumpton might not attract your attention as you drive by on the B5411. After all, it looks like a typical English country church. But most people don't realise that buried in the grounds of this particular church is a notorious Lancashire witch who put so much fear into the local population that they took action to fortify her grave to prevent her ever coming back from the dead.

Meg Shelton lived in the area at the end of the 17th century, a time when formal charges of witchcraft were on the wane. Had she lived a few decades earlier – at the time of the Pendle Witches, say (page 149) – then her fate in this county may well have been different.

Meg set up home in the Lancashire countyside, frequenting a range of rural settlements and becoming known throughout the area. Rumoured to possess a range of supernatural powers, she earnt the rather unbecoming and unpleasant nickname 'the Fylde Hag'. Meg was a cunning woman, known for her abilities to heal maladies using herbal remedies, but she also had a reputation for darker abilities, such as casting spells. Local hardships were blamed on her 'witchcraft'; she was accused of being responsible for secretly and magically stealing milk when the dairy farmer's entire herd of cows stopped producing. Illness among cattle also saw fingers pointed at her, while others accused her of shapeshifting and appearing in the form of various animals. These eccentric claims saw Meg become one of the most famous Lancashire witches.

This reputation did not fade when Shelton died, reportedly crushed against the wall of a barn while trying to steal corn. In fact, the legend of the Woodplumpton Witch posthumously spiralled to terrify villagers long after her burial. Stories started to spread about the Fylde Hag clawing her way out of the grave and haunting those who upset her during life. It's said that the corpse was found above ground in the churchyard at least twice. Some claim her motivation for rising from the grave was simply to cause mischief. So concerned were the local community, they had the body reburied, with Shelton buried head first and a large glacial boulder placed on top of the grave. It was believed witches could get out of their final resting place unless there was a barrier to keep them underground. The boulder remains, with a memorial plaque next to it.

The witch's grave at St Anne's Church has plenty of visitors, from those with a fascination for the paranormal to those with a nose for curious local history. It's not unusual to see flowers left here as a mark of respect for a woman who endured more than her fair share of problems and accusations during her life – troubles that continued well after her death.

ST ANNE'S CHURCH, WOODPLUMPTON RD, WOODPLUMPTON, PRESTON, PR4 ONE

BELOW The stone placed to keep the 'Fylde Hag' under the ground.

70 Samlesbury Hall, Preston, Lancashire

Step back in time and embark on a Victorian ghost hunt in this Lancashire hall, which has plenty of spirits dwelling within

Working out which hall, pub or castle is the most haunted in the country is a tall task, but Samlesbury Hall should definitely make your shortlist. At the latest count, there are thought to be no fewer than 13 ghosts haunting this hall, an unlucky number of spooks. One of them, though, gets more attention than the rest. This is the phantom of Lady Dorothea Southworth, a former resident of Samlesbury Hall who experienced much tragedy. The legend associated with her ghost has its roots in love, as so many do. Lady Dorothea, it is said, fell in love with the young Richard de Hoghton, who hailed from a neighbouring village. But he was a Protestant, and couples simply could not go out courting if they had religious differences. After all, this was during Elizabethan times, when the tension between Catholics and Protestants was off the charts. But, in a precursor to Romeo and Juliet, the lovestruck couple were not going to let God get in the way of their love, and they decided to run away together.

However, all did not go according to plan. The pair planned to elope on Christmas Eve, but news of the marriage reached Dorothea's father and he tried to put a stop to it. A man was sent to murder Richard and two of his companions. The bodies were dragged away and buried in the grounds of Samlesbury Hall. Dorothea witnessed this shocking act and was sent to a convent in France. The story of Dorothea, who has been known to appear

ABOVE Samlesbury Hall has an appearance that just screams 'haunted house'.
OPPOSITE Inside the haunted hall.

as the 'Lady in White', is told to visitors in what is now called the Ghost Room. This spooky place is found in the attic and, incredibly, was opened up for the first time in 700 years in autumn 2023.

Salmesbury Hall takes its ghosts very seriously and is keen for members of the public to come along and participate in activities that involve being in the places where hauntings have happened. Staff also keep a detailed database of every event that has taken place there over the centuries, be it a sighting, feeling of energy or mysterious sound. Those who have been through such encounters are encouraged to fill out a form on their website to say exactly what took place, then it can be matched up to other paranormal happenings within this historic building.

Those brave enough can even take part in a Torchlight Tour. In darkened surroundings in the dead of night, take your torch around the corridors and rooms of this hall and try to tap into the spirit world. Your guide will have plenty of stories on hand about the ghosts dwelling here and how they have appeared, frightened folk and caused mischief over the decades.

Hardcore supernatural explorers may also want to step back in time to take part in the Great Victorian Ghost Hunt. This one is a real gem because all the modern, hi-tech equipment you see on various TV shows (teams from *Most Haunted* and *Ghost Hunters International* have undertaken investigations here) are abandoned in favour of 19th-century ghost-hunting tools. This makes for an even creepier experience as you tentatively tread your way around the hall's haunted nooks and crannies. This is ghost hunting at its scariest!

Samlesbury Hall does not shy away from its haunted reputation. Rather it embraces it, and encourages you to do the same.

PRESTON NEW RD, SAMLESBURY, PRESTON, PR5 0UP
WWW.SAMLESBURYHALL.CO.UK

71 The Blackpool Tower Dungeon, Blackpool, Lancashire

Enter this immersive underground world, led by a talented troupe of petrifying performers

Away from the rides and the piers, the ice creams and the chip shops, an experience awaits that will have you grimacing – and maybe blurting out a scream or two. All in good fun, of course.

Blackpool is home to one of the most marvellous dungeon experiences run by Merlin Entertainments, blending fact-filled history with theatrical thrills. It's *Horrible Histories* in the flesh, with added jump scares and gore thrown in to keep you on your toes. If you're brave enough to see it through and game enough to take part in some interactive jesting, you're going to learn a lot about the history of Lancashire down the centuries. You may have heard of some characters before, like the Pendle Witches (page 149), but there's plenty here that will be new to you. Some of it may even keep you awake at night...

You'll first get to grips with the history of the Fylde Coast, covering events from centuries past that had a troubling impact on the local population – Viking invasions and the War of the Roses included. You'll meet a fearful monk, suspicious of outsiders in case they brought the plague to these parts and certainly not in the mood to offer anyone sanctuary. The plague did reach Lancashire, of course, and you'll learn about how it affected the

ABOVE Learn about gruesome Lancashire history at the Blackpool Dungeon.

population and what the hot cures of the time were.

The torture demo is always a favourite for those enjoying a dungeon experience, and for this one you're transported straight to Lancaster Castle's chamber. The 'torturer' will show you the tools of their trade and will be only too happy to give a demonstration about how they were used. He may ask for volunteers (if you're from neighbouring Yorkshire, I'd keep quiet about it). If you're a fan of the Killers, you might recognise this torture chamber. It was used in the video for their single 'Here With Me', which was directed by the master of all things strange, Tim Burton.

After a brief encounter with two local body-snatchers who used to steal corpses from graves in order to make a quick buck, you're off to meet Alizon Device. She's one of the most famous names in the Lancashire paranormal world – one of the original Pendle Witches. With witchcraft reports through the roof in the 17th century, it seems nobody was safe from being accused. The hunt for witches could even have led to your door. It certainly led to Alizon's. And so, standing in front of you, the fully costumed witch explains what it was like for her at the time, the effects of being at the centre of a witch hunt, and what happened to her and her fellow accused at Lancaster Castle. Few experiences bring history to life in such a vivid, fun way, and you may well learn more about Lancashire history during your visit than you would in any other museum – even if your heart is racing and you spend half the time grabbing on to your friends for comfort.

BELOW Blackpool is the ideal place for the theatrical and macabre.

TOWER ENTRANCE, BANK HEY STREET, BLACKPOOL, FY1 4BJ
WWW.THEDUNGEONS.COM/BLACKPOOL

72 The Rock-Cut Graves, Heysham, Lancashire

Visit a mysterious set of graves cut into the rock of an atmospheric clifftop

Despite being home to a nuclear power station and a port where ferries depart for the Isle of Man, Heysham manages to retain a quaint, picturesque side with its narrow, sloping streets, cosy cottages and stunning views. The village reaches optimum charm in the area around St Peter's Church, a tiny and stunning place of worship with an incredible backdrop of Morecambe Bay and the distant Lake District. But go a little beyond it, out onto the paths winding across the clifftop, and you'll come across one of the strangest graves in the country. The Heysham rock-cut graves have alarmed visitors and baffled historians in equal measure. Visit in the evening as the sun sets over the bay and the sense of mystery is all the more heightened. This can be an unsettling place, with some hearing voices in the wind seemingly whispering of spirits and ancient rituals.

What you'll see here, close to the ruined chapel of St Patrick's, are six shallow graves. But rather than being rectangular in shape, they have the outline of a human body. It's not hard to imagine bodies being placed inside these shapes, with the surrounding rock offering close-knit protection. The passing of time and all of its climes has weathered the stones, adding to the eerie nature of the graves. And the more you discover about Heysham's rock-cut graves, the more mysterious they become. No records have been found to establish who might have been buried here. There are no inscriptions on or around the graves, and no remains were found. Maybe there were no bodies to begin with. Were these

RIGHT The mysterious clifftop graves had Ozzy Osbourne's approval.

graves symbolic or perhaps part of a ritual to honour the dead? We may never know for sure.

The location of the graves conjures up an incredibly spooky atmosphere, particularly if the weather plays its part. St Patrick's Chapel looms over the site, harbouring its own ancient tales of faith and death. Stand next to the graves and you'll be looking over Morecambe Bay, a huge area with treacherous tides that also has many tragic stories to tell. When the howling wind blows in from the west, a sea mist hovers above the bay and the waves are crashing against the shore, this place takes on a Shakespearean quality, like a scene from *Macbeth*. Heavy metal rock band Black Sabbath saw the potential of this location, choosing the rock-cut graves as the cover image for their greatest hits album, *The Best Of Black Sabbath*, released in 2000.

But the creepy quality of this north-west archaeological relic isn't confined to the graves; there have been ghostly sightings here, too. Some visitors have noted this area to have an oppressive energy with an unsettling atmosphere; it's easy enough to imagine, with the stillness of the graves seeming out of place amid the wild weather that often hits this shoreline. Some claim to have heard voices on the wind blowing in from Morecambe Bay, while others suggest a monk is haunting the area. Maybe you'll see the figure, gazing out to sea in a forlorn manner, dressed in tatty clothing and emanating a sense of sorrow.

MAIN ST, HEYSHAM,
LA3 2RN

73 Lancaster Castle, Lancashire

Visit the place where the notorious Pendle Witches were tried and sentenced to death

The Pendle Witch Trials that took place in Lancaster in 1612 are perhaps the most famous of the witch-hunt era. They are to the UK what the 1629 Salem Witch Trials are to the United States. But while Salem has developed a massive tourist industry linked to their trials, complete with museums and Halloween hysteria, in Lancaster you still have to go out of your way to learn about the Pendle Witches. OK, the Salem Witch Trials were on a much larger scale, but the point is still valid. While there is a Pendle Witch Trail vaguely crossing Lancashire, much more could be made of this significant historical event. So, it is at Lancaster Castle where there is most to learn about the Pendle Witches, what exactly they were accused of and what happened to them. Book your tour in advance and you'll get to visit the cells and courtroom of this amazing building in the heart of the city.

The Pendle Witch story begins, funnily enough, out in rural Lancashire, near Pendle Hill. That's how they got their name, believe it or not. A group of people, mostly women, were accused of practising witchcraft. The evidence for this was sketchy at best, but among other things locals said was that they had cursed neighbours and caused the death of friends and family. They were brought before the court here in Lancaster Castle and faced a trial surrounded by suspicion, fear and hearsay. One of the most noted pieces of evidence came from nine-year-old Jennet Device, who made allegations against her own family members. And largely on the back of what this child said, 10 out of the 12 people on trial were found guilty and hanged on nearby Lancaster Moor. This was not an unusual outcome for this court, renowned as being a hotspot for capital punishment; for some periods in history, only judges at the Old Bailey in London sentenced more people to death. On the tour, you'll see the cells where the accused were held and the room in which they were kept before being led to the gallows. There's also a grim branding iron which was used on those convicted until 1811.

Third-party companies run ghost hunts in the castle if a daytime visit is not enough to quench your supernatural thirst. Those tours have thrown up some disturbing evidence of spooky events, including hushed whispers and footsteps in the courtroom, piercingly high noises and blue orbs seen where the Pendle Witches were held before their trial. Aside from the witches, there's also a monk said to haunt these grounds. He was another to be hanged and those seeing him recall an ice-cold chill in the air.

The castle was used as a prison right up until 2011. Some inmates and prison officers talk of seeing the apparition of a young girl and an older woman with a haggard appearance. And many ghost hunts focus on the Well Tower, where the ghost of convicted Pendle Witch Old Demdyke is thought to roam. She died in one of the cells during the trials in 1612. In fact, much of the activity recorded by ghost hunters in this part of the castle is thought to be down to her.

CASTLE HILL, LANCASTER, LA1 1YN
WWW.LANCASTERCASTLE.COM

BELOW The formidable fortress that is Lancaster Castle.

74 In Search of Dracula, Whitby, North Yorkshire

Enjoy a day walking in the shadow of the notorious Transylvanian count

With its historic winding streets, atmospheric ruined abbey, plethora of old pubs and a snarly, rugged coastline, Whitby is definitely one of the most ghostly places you can visit in England. Factor in the connections to one of the most famous Gothic horror stories ever written, and Whitby's place in *Spooky Britain* is well deserved. When Bram Stoker wrote *Dracula* in the 1890s he was influenced by many different locations, but Whitby is one of the places named and this atmospheric seaside town plays a pivotal role in the tale of the bloodthirsty count.

ABOVE Shiny abbey people: seeking out the literary legend of Dracula.

The first part of *Dracula* sees Jonathan Harker heading off to meet the titular vampire in Transylvania, before helping him to acquire property in England. Things take a dark turn and the count ends up on the Russian ship *Demeter*, bound for Whitby. He first makes an appearance in England in the form of a black dog when he jumps onto Tate Hill Pier. After killing all the crew, of course – perfectly standard behaviour for hungry, hungry vampires.

Other nearby places featured in the 19th-century novel include Whitby Abbey, which dominates the town's skyline from its position high on the east cliff, and the 199 steps leading up to St Mary's Church that have proved to be a measure of a pilgrim's determination to worship over the centuries. The entire town has grown to be a full part of the Dracula legend and so you're likely to see souvenirs in shops linked to the book and its many film and TV adaptions. Other books, such as the student favourite *Room 13*, have also picked up on the spooky vibe of Whitby and taken it in new directions. To get the most out of Whitby's connections with the evil Count Dracula, book onto one of the walking tours that explore all the locations in the town (www.whitbywalks.com/in-search-of-dracula). With a costumed guide looking like they've stepped straight out of the pages written by Bram Stoker, you'll hear stories connected to Dracula, while there's sure to be a few extra hair-raising happenings thrown in for good measure. Of course, make sure you read the story before you visit, or at least download it on spine-tingling audiobook.

During the day, head for the Dracula Experience (www.draculaexperience.co.uk). You'll find it on Marine Parade alongside the harbour. The attraction is in the building where Bram Stoker is thought to have written some of his famous book. There'll be creepy noises enticing you in if you have the stomach for a scare or two. Expect some jumps and a few slightly scary displays, all based around the legendary vampire who travelled across Europe and wreaked havoc on the folk of North Yorkshire and southern England. The history of the novel is also explored here, along with background information from Romania about the actual count, castle and vampire tales that inspired Stoker's tale. The cobbled, dimly lit streets of Whitby helped that Gothic author to pen his classic, and no doubt you'll enjoy the chilling atmosphere they can conjure up.

BOOK ONLINE; TOURS LEAVE FROM WEST CLIFF, WHITBY, YO21 3HA
WWW.WHITBYWALKS.COM/IN-SEARCH-OF-DRACULA

BELOW Stairway to Heaven: Whitby's steep steps lead up to the ruined abbey.

75 Whitby Goth Weekend, North Yorkshire

Step into a fun weekend of fashion and music inspired by Victorian Gothic horror and steampunk

Wondering when to explore Whitby and get to grips with its vampiric connections and haunting abbey views? Well, if you're really wanting to throw yourself into the experience and embrace the town's Gothic atmosphere, you simply must get involved in the Whitby Goth Weekend. Held twice a year, it's a fun event to take part in. But it's also quite the spectacle for those just here to watch. What started off as a small, cult event in the mid-1990s has now grown into one of the biggest goth festivals of the year. People come from all over to experience this extravaganza in what many consider to be the home of Count Dracula.

And so if you come to Whitby during the festival weekend – one held in spring and one in autumn – you'll see dozens and dozens of folk dressed up in the most elaborate Victorian, gothic and steampunk garb. Many of the costumes are simply exquisite and must have taken so long to perfect. Most folk are happy to pose for pictures; they've gone to a lot of effort to look the part and they're generally happy to take the praise and grab some attention. And it's the people, the Count Dracula cosplayers, that make this event so special. It really is

BELOW Good goth: the themed Whitby weekends bring out the best in spooky cosplay.

something to marvel at. You'll be walking by the side of the harbour or up the steps to the ruined abbey and see a host of Draculas, the odd Mina Harker and a wealth of other Victorian garb. Anything vaguely horror related, anything spooky, is lovingly adopted. And if you're reading this thinking you might like to spend the weekend dressed up as your very own Count Dracula, then go for it! You'll be in good company – during the festival weekends it's the people in 'normal' clothing that tend to stand out!

When darkness falls, the festival really hits its stride. The streets adopt a more mysterious air and it's quite bizarre coming across the Count on a dimly lit cobbled street after sunset. This is a music event, too, with gothic-themed bands playing at various venues in the town. There's even a special market place set up for you to buy any last-minute steampunk apparel and goth gear.

The backdrop to this fantastic event, of course, is one of the spookiest towns in the country. Whitby oozes ghost stories at every turn, from tales of phantom ships out on the misty sea to stories of spectral monks in the abbey and anecdotes of strange occurrences at the town's historic pubs. Hang out around Whitby Abbey and the old Black Horse Inn if you want to find a real chill in the air. There's so much paranormal activity said to occur in Whitby throughout the year; the gothic festival amplifies that mysterious atmosphere tenfold.

VARIOUS SITES ACROSS WHITBY
WWW.WHITBYGOTHWEEKEND.CO.UK

76 The Claife Crier, Windermere, Cumbria

Climbing this Lake District hill may bring you within earshot of a noisy ghost officially recognised by Ordnance Survey

On the western side of England's largest lake, a wooded hill rises to a peak and harbours a ghostly tale that has lived on in Cumbria for centuries. Those heading to the summit of Claife Hill will enjoy stunning views of Windermere and the rest of the Lake District. But lend an ear, my friend, lend an ear, for you may well hear an eerie sound belonging to a long-dead monk who still patrols these tree-lined shores. He's known as the 'Craife Crier' and if you look on your OS map, you will notice – bizarrely – that his haunted realm gets a mention in the woodland to the north of the hill. Now, the cartographers wouldn't lie about this kind of thing, would they? Absolutely not. So when hiking round these parts, I always make sure I keep my wits about me, as well as a backpack and sturdy shoes. There are those who reckon this is the only ghost to feature on an OS map, but you've read the chapter on Lost Lad too, right (page 122)?

The spirit accused of making such an unholy noise in the Lake District is said to belong to a monk who lived at Furness Abbey in the 12th century. So the tale goes,

ABOVE Some refused to go on the water after hearing the dramatic sound of the crier.

this monk was walking with a beautiful woman he had fallen in love with, but alas his love was unrequited, and she rejected him. He continued walking on his own, but his body, heart and mind were now broken; he collapsed and died soon after. His sorry soul remained in the woods around Craife Hill, though, and his desperately sad wailing has been heard in the area on several occasions down the centuries.

The sorrowful sounds became the stuff of legend in Victorian times, when ghost stories were becoming increasingly captivating. Several accounts appeared in local newspapers at the time. Ferrymen operating boats between the eastern and western shores of Windermere sometimes refused to land if the screams were being made, so terrifying were they. One night in 1852 there was a new ferryman who didn't believe the stories of the monk's wailing. He set off in turbulent weather, believing there was somebody on the western side in urgent need of safe passage over the water. The ferryman returned to the eastern shore without a passenger, but he did bring back with him all the signs of a traumatic ghostly encounter. He became severely ill and died within a couple of days, having refused to speak a work about what had happened on his last voyage across the lake. We may never know what horrors he experienced.

After these events, there grew a certain panic among the local population and it's believed some people took part in an exorcism in the woods at the far side of the lake, in an attempt to rid the area of the terrible hauntings. The mysterious ceremony succeeded according to local legend. Well, sort of. The locals reckon they heard fewer cases of wailing across the water following the exorcism, but the problem was not entirely solved. Legend has it the spirit was banished to a disused quarry that sits in a quiet corner of those mysterious woods. It's been quieter since it was restricted to that smaller area, according to the story and much to the relief of the ferrymen who were operating at the time. But it's not been completely silenced. Some walkers strolling through the woods in the northern approach to Craife Hill have reported strange sounds on the wind, perhaps a mournful moaning from the crier. Reports have often coincided with misty weather and poor visibility, but ghostly figures have also been spotted among the trees. Could it be that the monk – who gave up his vows for a love that never was – is still coming to terms with the rejection all these centuries later? Best take care on your stroll around these parts.

THE HILL CAN BE ACCESSED USING SEVERAL PATHS ON THE WESTERN SHORES OF WINDERMERE

BELOW Dead bodies were brought through here on the way to the burial ground.

77 The Lake District Corpse Roads, Cumbria

Follow the route used to transport the dead to their final resting place

As long as the wind and driving rain stay away, there are few places I'd rather be than trudging up a Lake District fell in anticipation of the incredible 360-degree view at the summit. Like thousands of other pilgrims to this amazing National Park, I'm on a mission to complete the 214 peaks known as the 'Wainwrights', after the author who described and illustrated them. At the time of writing, I've around 65 to go. My progress has been slow because these are difficult mountains to climb. Even the smaller of the summits involve challenging climbs and dangerous descents. It's hard enough work completing them carrying a bag

ABOVE Shap's church of St Michael.

packed with your lunch; what I could not imagine doing is hoisting a coffin or even a lightly wrapped dead body up onto the fells. But that's exactly what used to happen in centuries gone by, with some of these Lakeland tracks becoming known as 'Corpse Roads'.

These arduous journeys took place during medieval times and even into the 18th century – not because there was a desire to take the dead on one last scenic journey, but rather because of old religious laws that made the posthumous treks necessary. In those days, before reforms brought in new laws, only so-called 'mother churches' were allowed to bury the dead, meaning the bodies had to be brought to them from remote places in this mountainous landscape. The fastest routes were often over high-altitude passes – the Corpse Roads. With the help of local men and pack ponies, these journeys must have been grim. Several sprang up and, given they were often used at night and pallbearers struggled on by candlelight, unsurprisingly they're now renowned for their mysterious atmosphere and ghostly sightings. Walking along a Corpse Road is tricky at the best of times, but it's something else entirely when you add a little mist, an eerie wind and you head out at dusk.

Corpse Roads can be found between Rydal and Grasmere and over hills from Wasdale to Eskdale. One of the best known of these historic trails culminates at Shap, on the eastern edges of the Lake District. Historically, Shap had its own abbey (you can still visit the spooky ruins) and so was high up the religious pecking order. The church of St Michael was one of those where burials were permitted and so anybody dying over the hill in Mardale had to be brought across the fells to Shap. The rules were changed in 1729 to finally allow burials in Mardale. But there is a grim irony to the story; even those who were buried in Mardale had to have their bodies transported to and reburied in Shap when the valley was flooded to create the Haweswater Reservoir in the 1930s. Look for the graves near the railway line in the churchyard.

You can still wander along this ancient Corpse Road, but beware – ghost hunters have reported some strange goings-on, including wispy patterns forming, the feeling of hands pressing down on them and whispering on the wind. A particular hotspot for paranormal activity seems to be the larger boulders, which were used for resting while carrying the corpses along their final journey. Some say there's a concentration of spiritual energy at these points and you can feel people watching you. Maybe don't walk it alone!

KELD LN, SHAP, CA10 3NB

78 Castlerigg Stone Circle, Keswick, Cumbria

Take a trip to a hill above Keswick where a mysterious stone circle stands, wrapped in local myth and legend

From the centre of the Lake District tourist hotspot of Keswick, Castlerigg Stone Circle is either a short drive or a 30-minute walk. Whichever you opt for, you won't regret adding this mysterious ancient feature to your itinerary. Unless, that is, there's driving rain in a howling storm, something there's a good chance of in these parts, though should probably be avoided, because this spooky destination at the top of a hill is extremely exposed to the elements. Far better to save this one for a sunny day, and for maximum effect you should head here at sunrise or dusk. Both the rising and setting sun cast fascinating shadows, and it's at these times that paranormal activity has been most frequently reported.

Dating back 5,000 years, and historians still having no certainty as to why it was placed here, Castlerigg Stone Circle has amassed more than its fair share of myth and legend over the centuries, like many other of our stone circles. And, because of its location, you can gain access to the stone circle at any time and get up close to the stones. Touching these ancient rocks and enjoying the stunning Cumbrian scenery that surrounds them certainly gets you wondering who else has been here over the millennia, why these stones were placed here and just what scenes they have witnessed. There are 38 stones, some standing 1.5m (5ft) tall and others long since toppled to the ground. Archaeologists reckon there could have been 41 stones here at one point, making this one of the largest and best-preserved stone circles in the UK.

BELOW Some of the finest views in the Lake District are from Castlerigg Stone Circle.

A common sighting in these mysterious stone circles the world over has been strange, magical lights dancing around the stones. One such tale provides Castlerigg with a very spooky story. It dates back to 1919, when a group of male friends walked up to the stone circle one night. What they saw shocked them and could not be explained. Balls of light were dancing over the stones, swaying steadily and slowly. This strange phenomenon is a rarity, but people on 'Team Believer' say it's likely to be due to the latent energy associated with the stones and their meaningful layout.

Other local legends have grown up around Keswick's famed stone circle. Some Cumbrians talk about the stones moving or disappearing and then reappearing. Others have reported going to the site on different days and counting a different number of stones, yet not being able to explain it. The weather in the Lake District is notoriously changeable, and when mists suddenly creep across the stone circle it adds a certain chill to the scene – perhaps this influenced their counting of the stones? Yet, some folk have reported mists bizarrely appearing on photographs taken on perfectly clear days. Who do you believe?

Despite the strange happenings, this is a spiritual spot, somewhere people come to find peace and remember loved ones who once also found solace in this special location. It's common to find flowers placed at the foot of the stones, loving tributes that add to the mystery and haunting nature of this countryside henge.

CASTLE LN, KESWICK, CA12 4RN

79 The Cursing Stone of Carlisle, Cumbria

Read the words once uttered by a Scottish archbishop to invoke misfortune on raiders

The pedestrian subway close to Carlise's Tullie Museum is certainly not one of the city's most picturesque areas, though it is perhaps an appropriate spot for something as strangely dark and devilish as an ancient curse. Inscribed here on an attractive piece of granite rock known as the Cursing Stone is a selection of words from a detailed and complex historic curse. The street art was produced by artist Gordon Young as part of a regeneration project. Some say the Cursing Stone – part of a larger public artwork trail – is a fabulous addition to the city's artistic heritage; others contend that it's reopening old wounds that should have been long healed...

The curse was originally invoked by the Archbishop of Glasgow, Gavin Dunbar, in 1525. It targeted the Border Reivers – raiders who were operating in the borderlands during the Middle Ages, invoking fear and panic among those living there. The curse was extremely detailed. Obviously a lot of thought went into it because it ran for 1,069 words (a small part of it is captured on the Cursing Stone).

To summarise, then, the curse called for divine wrath to be unleashed upon the Border Reivers. It condemned the crimes they were accused of, including theft and violence, and then went on to invoke misfortune on every aspect of their lives and harm upon their health. It even asked for harm to come to their descendants and for their livelihoods to be ruined. Pretty harsh stuff, though maybe to be expected given the strength of feeling. And let's not forget that this was the Middle Ages, after all, when the fear of God counted for an awful lot. The curse was repeated regularly from the pulpits in churches all over the borderlands, where land was disputed and the Reiver families were renowned for creating havoc. And the granite stone is not the only memorial to this troubled region's past; the names of some of the Reiver families are inscribed at the entrance.

Curiously enough, the Cursing Stone stoked up controversy when it was installed in 2001 as part of the city's millennium celebrations. Even though it included the words uttered by a man of the cloth, it unnerved some locals, who were worried that unnatural forces were being encouraged. And in the months and years following the unveiling of the stone, the city went through some challenging times. Floods affected many areas, causing millions of pounds of damage. Foot and mouth disease arrived, ravaging local farms, and factories closed. I contacted Gordon Young when writing this book and he said the stone had even been blamed for Carlise United being relegated from the English Football League (die-hard fans will often look for something or someone to blame rather than dodgy defending and poor finishing…). Some superstitious folk – including a city councillor – even called for the stone to be removed for the sake of the town's prosperity. But it remains in place to this day as a kind of curious and morbid reminder of the turbulent history in this region.

CARLISLE
WWW.GORDONYOUNG.INFO

BELOW The controversial Cursing Stone in the centre of Carlisle.

80 The Poison Garden at Alnwick, Northumberland

Enjoy a walk around the most dangerous garden in the country – just don't touch anything!

When you visit a professionally kept garden, there is a certain expectation of what you'll find there. The smell of the roses in summer, the vibrant colours exploding from bulbs in the spring, the exquisitely designed lawns, the waterfalls that add that little bit extra... What you might not anticipate while walking among the daffodils and dahlias is the risk of a slow and painful death if you get too close to the flora! The Alnwick Garden has all the usual attractions green-fingered tourists are looking for, but with one unique and very dark addition – the Poison Garden. Lurking behind a pair of sturdy black gates and some very clear warning signs is a deadly world of mysterious plants that could do you some serious harm. Proceed with caution.

Beware the first golden rule: You're not allowed to go in on your own. It's that serious. To experience the Poison Garden you need to enter with an expert on one of the site's extremely informative and fascinating tours. The plants in the Poison Garden can kill, make no mistake about that. There are around 100 plant species in here and they're all either toxic, intoxicating or narcotic. You'll be warned not to touch, smell or taste any of them. Within the protected area inside the deadly garden you'll find laburnum, giant hogweed, opium poppy and atropa belladonna. Because of the toxicity of some of these plants, it's not surprising to learn some unsavoury people have tried to use them for chilling purposes. The guide will fill you in on some of the

more sinister cases involving attempted murders using plant-based poison. And some more surprising cases are also reported – such as a poisoning that took place because a toxic bush was cut from a garden, bagged up and placed in the confinement of a car on the way to the dump. The driver had a narrow escape...

There's also a practical element to the tour; you know, just in case you find yourself stuck out in the wild. You'll discover what you can and cannot forage in the woods. Being able to correctly identify species of fungi could literally be the difference between life and death out in the wilderness.

And if you can't get enough of this poisonous experience, head to the shop and buy the book highlighting every terrifying species you've just discovered, along with information about how deadly they are. Or take home some Poison Garden gin and vodka. Tours leave every 30 minutes and are limited to 20 people.

The Alnwick Garden is not far from Alnwick Castle, another place of magic, mystery and intrigue, as this stunning place stood in for Hogwarts School of Witchcraft and Wizardry in the early *Harry Potter* films. It's worth popping by for a bit of wizardry and witchery; kids can even learn how to fly a broomstick! You need to pay separately for Alnwick Garden (which the Poison Garden is inside), which became a major visitor attraction in the Northwest when it was given a serious makeover at the turn of the 21st century. Created by the Duchess of Northumberland, the modern garden has sculptures, incredible plants and some stunning water features, which make it a tremendous family day out. You'll see the largest collection of European plants in the UK here, as well as the largest Japanese cherry orchard in the world. All incredible stuff, but it's the Poison Garden and all of its perilous plant life that leaves a truly lasting impression...

DENWICK LANE, ALNWICK, NE66 1FJ
WWW.ALNWICKGARDEN.COM

LEFT The Poison Garden in Alnwick Gardens is not to be trifled with.

81 Chillingham Castle, Northumberland

Pluck up the courage to stay in a haunted suite or embark on a ghost tour in one of the UK's most haunted castles

This 12th-century stronghold became fully fortified as Chillingham Castle in 1344 and the family living there during this period can be traced all the way from that day to this. Throughout the centuries, the strategically placed and historic Chillingham Castle has hosted royal visitors, withstood attacks, witnessed border battles and seen no fewer than 18 castle generals made Knights of the Garter. With a long history of gruesome goings-on, it's little wonder that Chillingham is now known as one of the most haunted historic castles in the country. Ghost-hunting television shows regularly film here, so there is clearly a lot of action to behold. And there are plenty of opportunities for you to get involved with this spooky site. But just who, or what, are the spirits giving this castle its ghostly reputation?

BELOW The castle is lovely by day, but changes character after sunset (opposite).

Several phantoms are said to wander the castle, their spirits trapped inside this formidable building over centuries. The most famous of these is the 'Radiant Boy', a child-like spectre seen in the Pink Room and linked to bones that were found in the walls. From time to time, people have sworn they heard the cries of the boy on the stroke of midnight. Some say they come across as cries of pain, with others claiming the boy sounds fearful. Either way, it must be an alarming sound to hear, though I imagine it's made considerably worse for those involved when they see a bright halo of light atop a small figure dressed in blue. Imagine you've been woken by this noise while staying overnight in the Pink Room, and you open your eyes to see the Radiant Boy moving towards you...!

If spooky boys aren't enough to get your heart racing, then how about spurned brides? Lady Berkeley was devastated when her husband, Lord Grey, ran off with her sister, Lady Henrietta. It's said you can hear the rustle of Lady Berkeley's dress as she sweeps the corridor looking for her husband, leaving a cold chill in the air.

Along with moans being heard in the castle dungeon, where gruesome suffering was once endured, and the sightings of ghostly soldiers once stationed here, I'm sure you'll agree Chillingham Castle is a hotbed of paranormal activity. So, have you got what it takes to spend the night here or actually go in search of one of the ghosts?

The castle fully embraces its reputation as a place for ghostly encounters by inviting guests to stay overnight in a range of different suites. Some of them are more haunted than others. But if you're not sure you'd get 40 winks on account of keeping one eye open all night, then fear not; there are tours available several times a week that take you into the castle and grounds, picking out the places where sightings have taken place. A guide adds a spine-tingling narrative all the way. The tours last two hours and you need to book in advance, but there's also a four-hour ghost hunt option, in which you'll take part in a hands-on operation to seek out the Chillingham spooks. Whichever option you go for, there's a lot of creepy fun to be had at this amazing castle set in the beautiful Northumberland countryside.

CHILLINGHAM CASTLE, CHILLINGHAM, ALNWICK, NORTHUMBERLAND, NE66 5NJ
WWW.CHILLINGHAM-CASTLE.COM

82 Bamburgh Castle, Northumberland

Venture inside this formidable coastal fortress and you may chance upon one of the many ghosts said to reside here

The village of Bamburgh is small, quaint and home to some lovely little tea rooms, so it's a little surprising when you arrive at the castle. At first it seems out of place. It's a vast, visually stunning fortress and has been important since the Anglo-Saxon period, when it was the royal seat of the kings of Northumbria. Back then, it was a wooden structure. The sturdier stone structure was developed by the Normans in the 11th century. The stronghold has witnessed Viking invasions and played an important role in the War of the Roses, but it started to fall into disrepair in the 18th and 19th centuries. Fortunately, it was in the hands of wealthy industrialist William Armstrong by the end of the 19th century, and he spent a fortune to get it fully restored.

To truly appreciate the full beauty of Bamburgh Castle, go for a walk along the beach. As you're stood on the long stretch of sand, the impressive fortress ahead of you is flanked by the North Sea on one side and dunes on the other. No wonder this was voted one of the best views in Britain following a BBC survey. This amazing backdrop has even been the setting for an *Indiana Jones* film (*The Dial of Destiny*). But it's not all just serene setting, picture-perfect photographs or rugged archaeologists. For Bamburgh has a storied and often dark history, featuring bloody battles and desperate prisoners held captive in deep, dingy dungeons. No surprise, then, to learn this is a must-visit if you're into all things spooky.

The two most famous ghosts living in Bamburgh Castle belong to women, each known by the different-coloured clothes they wear. Let's take a look at

BELOW Rattling chains and painful moans have been heard by visitors to Bamburgh Castle.

the 'Pink Lady' first of all, seen several times floating along the halls in a pink gown that flows out behind her. Some have claimed to feel a drop in temperature as she appears, with others hearing weeping from this sad soul. Legend has it the spectre belongs to a young woman who fell in love with a knight who was based at the castle. But her father wouldn't have her kicking about with the likes of him. Tragically, the heartbroken woman threw herself from the castle walls when she was wrongly told her beloved had died. Another lady to haunt the corridors of Bamburgh Castle wears a green cloak. Visitors report seeing flashes of green and objects move around on their own. While the Pink Lady tends to be mournful, the 'Green Lady' has a much more mischievous streak.

The ghost of Dr John Sharp is also thought to be present. He spent much time and money renovating the castle and saving it from ruin, so has an obvious interest in keeping a watchful eye on things.

All good castles have the legend of a ghost in a suit of armour, and Bamburgh is no exception. Standing on the battlements, looking out over the castle, the knight is said to have fallen in combat, forever destined to remain in the place he was defending. Listen carefully. You may hear the sound of clanking metal armour as he surveys the grounds.

If you head to Bamburgh at Halloween, you can take part in the ghostly tours that show you around the creepiest parts of the castle. The dungeons, however – perhaps the grimmest experience of all – can be explored all year round. Prisoners held here often died due to harsh treatment. Many poor souls were executed here, too. Rattling chains have been heard, as well as painful moans. It's said to be the most haunted part of the castle, so if you're into the paranormal, venturing down here is a necessary evil.

BAMBURGH, NE69 7DF
WWW.BAMBURGHCASTLE.COM

83 Alloway Auld Kirk, South Ayrshire
84 Glasgow Necropolis, Glasgow
85 Edinburgh Castle, Edinburgh
86 The Blair Street Underground Vaults, Edinburgh
87 The Edinburgh Dungeon, Edinburgh
88 The Real Mary King's Close, Edinburgh
89 The Ghost Bus Tours, Edinburgh
90 The Arthur's Seat Coffins, Edinburgh
91 Scotland's Secret Bunker, nr St Andrews, Fife
92 Inveraray Jail, Argyll and Bute
93 Glencoe, Scottish Highlands
94 Massacre Cave, Isle of Eigg
95 Loch Ness, Drumnadrochit, Highland
96 Culloden Battle Site, nr Inverness, Highland

Scotland

83 Alloway Auld Kirk, South Ayrshire

Visit the churchyard mentioned in Robbie Burns' famous 'Tam o' Shanter' poem, where witches and warlocks made merry to the Devil's music

The birthplace of Scottish bard Robert Burns, Alloway provides the setting for one of his darkest and most spiritual pieces of work, 'Tam o' Shanter'. The poem's main event is a crazed dance by wizards and warlocks in the churchyard of the auld kirk in his hometown. Evidently a place for spooky happenings during the 18th century, the ruined church remains shrouded in intrigue and continues to attract all those with a fascination for the paranormal. The churchyard provides an eerie setting, the roofless kirk standing nearby and being notable for its two gable ends rising towards the sky in a lonely fashion.

The church was a ruin even back in the days when Scotland's much-loved poet was crafting his finest work. Burns wrote 'Tam o' Shanter' in 1790. It's a lengthy story about a local farmer who liked his drink and spent many a night getting wasted at the nearby hostelry. After one evening consuming too much alcohol at the pub, farmer Tam was riding his horse, Meg, back home to his long-suffering wife. Through the Scottish countryside they were speeding when Tam passed Alloway Auld Kirk. What he witnessed there was indeed a shocking and troubling sight; witches and warlocks were dancing wildly in the churchyard with the Devil providing the musical backing of bagpipes. The figures were mainly grotesque, and Tam – just like you or I – should really have just kept on going and made for home, perhaps never to speak of it again. But no. He saw a young witch he liked the look of – she was wearing a short skirt (called a 'cutty sark' by Burns), and Tam couldn't resist calling to her, the fool. All hell then breaks loose. Witches and

BELOW Alloway Auld Kirk, the subject of the famous Robert Burns poem.

spirits chase after Tam o' Shanter in a flurry of activity. He races away on Meg towards the river because folklore deems evil spirits unable to cross running water. Crossing a bridge, he just escapes with his life but poor Meg loses her tail as it's menacingly ripped off by a witch called Nannie. The poem is a warning about the effects of consuming too much ale. Take heed, although I note the writer and the poem are now celebrated on an annual basis with large quantities of whisky, especially on Burns Night in January.

Visiting this literary location is a spooky experience even during the daytime, especially if you have knowledge of the poem's narrative. The weathered ruin of the church sat before crumbling gravestones and the creaking ancient trees – it's the stuff of horror movies. The creepy occurrences have continued, too; there's talk locally of lights being seen near the auld kirk, and rumours of modern witches making hexes there. People have witnessed shadowy figures wandering around the ruins. Others claim to have heard sounds that include laughter or even strange chants. And were those galloping horse hooves that I heard? Others have reported them, too. Could this be Tam and Meg making a frenzied getaway? I'll drink a wee dram to them for making it.

ALLOWAY, AYR, KA7 4PQ
WWW.NTS.ORG.UK/VISIT/PLACES/ROBERT-BURNS-BIRTHPLACE-MUSEUM/HIGHLIGHTS/ALLOWAY-AULD-KIRK

84 Glasgow Necropolis, Glasgow

Explore the history of this great city through its huge, peaceful urban cemetery

A short walk from the bustling centre of Scotland's largest city, you'll find a thought-provoking hill that houses the bodies of over 50,000 Glaswegians. This is Glasgow's Necropolis, its City of the Dead. It's a strange site with a unique feel; the peaceful atmosphere provides a quiet place to reflect and admire the far-reaching views, while the Victorian statues and tombs undoubtedly add a haunting vibe. The 19th-century obsession with death and mourning is on show here for all to see in one of the most fascinating locations in all of urban Scotland. So atmospheric is the Glasgow Necropolis it's been chosen by many movie directors as an eye-catching location. Even Batman himself has ridden a motorbike through the Necropolis, with the eerie tombs providing a fitting film-noir backdrop for Gotham City. The Necropolis is also located next to Glasgow Cathedral, with the main route into it being across the elegant Bridge of Sighs that was once the sombre route of funeral processions.

The huge Necropolis was born out of the demand for more burial space. The city's population was growing, and so was the need to find more graves for its departed residents. Consecrated space was in big demand. And so, inspired by cemeteries already established in Paris, the Glasgow Necropolis was established in 1832. The desire for an attractive final resting place led to the Merchants' House of Glasgow buying the land and providing the city's distinguished citizens with a park-like environment for their final resting place. You'll be able to wander around the labyrinth of paths that wind their way up the hill and admire some of the 3,500 monuments that mark the graves, although the vast majority of the residents here didn't have the means for such grandeur.

You'll soon realise the finest sculptures and stonemasons were set to work on the tombs and monuments; they are intricate in their detail and visually stunning. One of the most famous is the John Knox Monument, a towering column dedicated to the 16th-century Scottish Reformation leader. It's at the highest point of the Necropolis and is a well-known landmark. Other key locations to visit include the grave of author William Miller, the man behind the nursery rhyme 'Wee Willie Winkie'. A grand mausoleum is dedicated to the industrialist Charles Tennant, who worked in the late 18th and early 19th centuries, and there is a domed tomb with fine carving and ironwork that is home to Major Archibald Douglas Monteath, an officer of the East India Company.

Even if you don't find the tombs of the most well-known people buried here, there are thousands of other monuments to raise your interest as you walk around this fascinating location. Although you may only cover a short distance, it's likely to take you a fair while because you just cannot help stopping regularly to read inscriptions and take photos. It's macabre, yes, but in a way it's beautiful. The labyrinth of pathways snake around the site, taking you through the maze of grave markers. To wander the site with an expert on an organised tour, search up the Friends of Glasgow Necropolis.

CASTLE ST, GLASGOW, G4 0UZ
WWW.GLASGOWNECROPOLIS.ORG

BELOW Glasgow's Necropolis is a fascinating yet sorrowful place to take a walk.

85 Edinburgh Castle, Edinburgh

Discover the dark history of Scotland's most famous castle – and the ghostly tales linked to it

Dominating the Edinburgh skyline and with a history as gruesome as it is lengthy, the castle at the top of the Royal Mile is a must-visit destination for anyone interested in macabre stories. Tales of troubled lives practically ooze from the stone walls which saw them take place, and you'll encounter them on every section of your tour through the castle, as you could well imagine of a fortress at the forefront of history for centuries.

It's in the older parts of the castle that the most famous spectre has been spotted. The 'Grey Lady' is quite a tragic ghost, crying as she wanders around the historic grounds. Some argue it could be the spectre of Janet Douglas, Lady Glamis, a woman accused of treason. Even though the claims were thought to be baseless, Janet was still burned to death outside the castle in July 1537, her son witnessing the horrific scene. No wonder the ghost is troubled.

Another well-known spooky sighting made around the castle is of a piper sent to explore the route of a newly discovered escape tunnel. He played his pipes so those following his progress could keep track of him. So, when the pipes fell silent, colleagues went to look for him. But the piper had vanished and the tunnel was sealed. Or so the story goes. However, if you're one of the folk who hears the faint sound of bagpipes on the Royal Mile, just strain your ears and decide for yourself if it's coming from underground.

One of the most torrid tales of Edinburgh Castle's past can be uncovered in the vaults below Crown Square. This was home to the castle's prison of war in the 18th and 19th centuries. The rooms have been recreated to show what it was like at the time, but it's barely possible to imagine the horrific discomfort experienced by the hundreds of people held here. The first prisoners were French and arrived when the Seven Years War broke out in 1758. The youngest inmate was just five – a drummer boy captured at the Battle of Trafalgar. Many soldiers fighting for American independence were also brought here. Before it was a prison of war, pirates from the Caribbean were held here, and many of them were hanged. Grisly tales come thick and fast, and the spirits of many souls still linger here.

One of the more surprising finds in the extensive grounds of the castle is a pet cemetery, the final resting place of many loyal canine companions who served soldiers based here. And a furry phantom is rumoured to be one of the ghostly apparitions you may encounter on your visit. Troubled tourists have seen what they described as a scruffy

OPPOSITE Edinburgh Castle: a beacon for Scottish supernatural stories.
OVERLEAF The spectres of Edinburgh Castle loom large all over the Scottish capital.

black dog scurrying around. I'm sure dog lovers will give it a friendly smile, should it be encountered.

Tickets for Edinburgh Castle can be booked online and you can self-tour with a guidebook or get involved with the audio tour. Take a look at the guided walk offered by Mercat Tours too, on which an expert storyteller paints a colourful picture of the castle's gruesome past.

CASTLEHILL, EDINBURGH, EH1 2NG
WWW.EDINBURGHCASTLE.SCOT AND WWW.MERCATTOURS.COM

86 The Blair Street Underground Vaults, Edinburgh

Enjoy an underground adventure into the history of crime and villainy

Edinburgh's South Bridge was built towards the end of the 18th century to connect the capital's old and new town, eliminating the need for well-to-do folk to go down the hill to the city's poorer streets. When it was built, the bridge contained a series of chambers beneath the surface that were initially used as workshops and shops; at the time the rent on these prestigious outlets was the highest in Europe. But there was a problem – they were not waterproof and, as any Scottish person will confirm, it tends to rain a lot up here. The vaults underneath the bridge became damp, cold and unsuitable, so were sealed up and forgotten about. That was not the end of their story, however.

Instead of being used as glitzy workplaces for creative Edinburgh

tradespeople, the vaults adopted a more sinister, unofficial use as a dark, hidden refuge for criminals and ne'er-do-wells. By the beginning of the 19th century, the murky transformation of these subterranean spaces was complete. Smugglers were attracted to the isolated 'no-go areas' and used them to store stolen goods and illegal alcohol. Prostitution was rife in the vaults, with some used as illegal brothels where violence against the women was a regular occurrence. It was not uncommon for people to be lured into the vaults, robbed and murdered. Other parts of the Blair Street Vaults became illegal drinking dens, attracting large groups of men and frequently seeing fights break out. And as the vaults were on the way to the medical schools at the university, it is rumoured that these hidden rooms were storage areas for those involved in body snatching. Recently buried bodies would be dug up in the early hours, stored here during the next day and taken to the medical schools when darkness fell again. There was seemingly no crime too hideous, no activity too macabre to be carried out in the vaults beneath this well-trodden bridge.

When this mysterious set of subterranean rooms and passageways was rediscovered by accident in the 1980s, it soon became a major tourist attraction and a popular haunt for local historians and ghost seekers.

BELOW In this Scottish city of ghosts, some of the more grisly history is found underground in the vaults.

Archaeologists had a field day examining the items left abandoned on the floor, from glass bottles to oyster shells. Every find helped piece together the spooky events that took place in the vaults once their intended use became so impractical.

Today, Mercat Tours provides your access to the vaults. Visit the website to book in on one of the popular ghost walks, which meets at the market cross on the Royal Mile and, taking in spooky stories along the way, head down to the entrance of this mysterious underground realm of horrors. Ghosts have been spotted inside this atmospheric and chilling location, with the guides – often hooded and always enthusiastic – telling convincing tales of sightings, blown-out candles and eerie noises in the darkened passageways. Pick your tour beneath the streets of Edinburgh carefully; the level of terrifying detail about historic events varies between each one. Some are family-friendly and others are strictly over-18s only. Check details on the website for the one that suits you. It all depends on the age of your group. Or how squeamish you are.

ABOVE These long-hidden passages were once home to crime and villainy.

BLAIR ST, EDINBURGH, EH1 1QR
WWW.MERCATTOURS.COM

87 The Edinburgh Dungeon, Edinburgh

See if you can survive this interactive tour into the ghastly past of Scotland's notoriously bloodthirsty capital city

Edinburgh is home to one of the spooky Dungeon attractions run by Merlin Entertainments, the company that also runs Alton Towers. Featuring live shows with convincing and entertaining actors, your ticket takes your small group through different periods of the city's history, all chosen to highlight the spooky and downright gory nature of this capital's past. Don't expect this to be a walk in the park; the tension, scares and chills in this popular, imaginative attraction can be too much for some people. But don't worry; there are opportunities to pull out along the way if it all gets a little too terrifying for you. On the flip side, there are also special tours just for adults if you feel you're able to handle an 18+ event, where they turn the jumps up to 11. The great thing about the different Dungeon experiences around the country is that they highlight the blood-stained history of that particular region, giving unique insights into the past. And there's plenty to delve into when you discover the creepy characters that once inhabited Edinburgh.

First up is the 17th-century courtroom where a mock trial shows you how rough justice was dished out in those days and what punishment criminals could expect to be handed down. And then you're off

RIGHT Expect a bloodthirsty dive into Edinburgh's history at the Dungeon.

to learn about Agnes Finnie, Edinburgh's most notorious witch, and how alleged witches were cruelly investigated by the witchpricker (a person paid to search accused individuals for a 'Devil's Mark' by pricking their skin with needles or pins to see if they were a spell maker or not). After learning about torture instruments, you'll enter Sawney Bean's Cannibal Cave, which is as horrendous as it sounds. In the 16th century, the Bean family loved having people round for dinner. The problem is that the guests were served up in broths rather than providing tableside chitchat. Few people know about this awkward part of Scottish history and it's a great way to find out about the country's cave-dwelling Hannibal Lecters.

My favourite on the tour is the encounter with Burke and Hare, the body-snatching duo who brought terror to Edinburgh in the early 19th century. This pair of hideous villains killed people and sold their bodies to doctors so they could carry out medical experiments. It's a fascinating and terrifying tale, and you'll even see recreations of the streets where these crimes took place.

In the Burke and Hare section of the Edinburgh Dungeon, as with everywhere else in the attraction, the attention to detail with the set, props and costumes is immense. The lighting and special effects add plenty to the experience, and there is even somebody in charge of making the smells in each zone authentic. There's also a ride to experience that comes packed with gallows humour. It's known as the Drop, and will have your stomach in knots. Sure, this is not a real dungeon. But if you're looking for a fun and scary trip back in time to gain a good understanding of the Scottish capital's history, the Edinburgh Dungeon is hard to beat.

MARKET STREET, EDINBURGH, EH1 1DF
WWW.THEDUNGEONS.COM/EDINBURGH

88 The Real Mary King's Close, Edinburgh

Delve beneath the streets of the Scottish capital to discover a rare – and truly spooky – insight into 17th-century life

The Royal Mile in Edinburgh is usually jam-packed with tourists enjoying the magical history and culture of this proud nation. But as visitors buy their whisky, stroll up to the castle and taste locally made fudge on this famous street, few are aware about a secret, creepy and mysterious world resting in timeless limbo beneath their feet. When the City Chambers were built in 1753, the development sealed off a number of once-thriving tenement blocks and streets beneath it to create what is in effect a massive time capsule. Arrange a tour at Real Mary King's Close and you'll walk into this preserved neighbourhood of yesteryear. You'll then be able to find out what it was like to live in the dimly lit alleys of Edinburgh during the 17th century. Named after local character Mary King, they are a snapshot of the capital's past that is now frozen in time.

ABOVE This tour beneath the city streets brings to life the filth and disease of Edinburgh's past.

Real Mary King's Close is well known as one of Edinburgh's top attractions. The costumed guides are expert storytellers and have plenty of tales to tell from down the centuries. And, to add to the chills, there's much talk of ghosts in this historic location – particularly in 'Annie's Room' where the spirit of a young girl is said to live. The presence here is so strong and the story so famous, some visitors bring soft toys for young Annie's ghost to play with. All the teddies make for an eerie sight. The story of this room came to light when renowned Japanese psychic Aiko Gibo arrived here to make a film about haunted places in the UK. She could barely enter the room, located off an old street called Allan's Close. Gibo said she felt the presence of a little child who haunts the room very strongly. She said the young girl was called Annie. Gibo communicated with the spirit by the fireplace and learnt that Annie had lost her favourite doll, making her very upset. So Gibo went to a shop on the Royal Mile and left her one, something visitors have been doing ever since. It's a creepy enough story as it is, but being in Annie's Room and seeing the piles of dolls near the fireplace raised the bar on the spookometer somewhat.

If you thought the ghoulish stories would end there, then think again. Practically every step of the Real Mary King's Tour involves some reference to grim history that has the potential to freak out the squeamish. One of the most grisly stories is linked to the plague and how the Plague Doctor – dressed in the nightmarish mask they thought deterred disease – visited victims in these very houses. It's an image that will stay with you for some time.

Wandering around these hidden, subterranean streets that were forgotten about for so many decades, it's easy to lose sense of being in the 21st century. From the moment you descend into this hidden Edinburgh underworld, you are travelling back to a time when the streets were riddled with disease, crime and poverty. Many of Edinburgh's former residents lived unhealthy, unhappy lives, and this is your opportunity to share in their misery should you so choose.

WARRISTON'S CL, EDINBURGH, EH1 1PG
WWW.REALMARYKINGSCLOSE.COM

RIGHT Toys brought to the room said to be haunted by a young ghost.

89 The Ghost Bus Tours, Edinburgh

Step inside a creepy double-decker and enjoy a spooky journey to all the best haunts in Scotland's capital

As soon as you see the black, mysterious Routemaster bus winding through Edinburgh's historic streets, it creates an urgency to get involved. The curious curtains adorning the windows, the eerie lamps lighting the interior, and the haunting signage announcing this to be the 'Ghost Bus' – it all combines to lure you aboard and treat you to a devilish tour of Edinburgh's paranormal hotspots. Although this is one of the famous fleet of buses that once ran commuters around London, once inside it you'll realise it's been totally and utterly transformed. It's more theatre than public transport, gothic décor and ghostly conductors producing a macabre atmosphere for a tour of spooky Edinburgh – all with a dark humour that grimly lightens the mood between scary stories. You'll definitely be kept on the edge of your seat during this ghostly adventure; flickering lights, hidden props, scary stories and screeching sounds will take care of that.

The key stops on the Ghost Bus Tour read like a list of the city's scariest sites. You'll see Edinburgh Castle (page 182), where sieges and executions have left a spiritual imprint. Below the castle walls, Grassmarket was once used for public hangings; many witches and criminals met a grisly end on these streets, watched by angry crowds. The Royal

Mile has been home to many sightings and reports of chilling whispers, while Holyrood Palace may be the Scottish home of the king but the ghost of a woman accused of witchcraft has been living their much longer – Agnes Simpson was executed here in the late 1500s.

The highlight of this creepy bus tour is Greyfriars Kirkyard, which has a reputation for being one of the most haunted graveyards in the world. It is certainly one of the spookiest places in Edinburgh. The bus stops here and you're invited to alight so you can stand in the kirkyard and listen to tales that have been reported down the decades. One of the most famous concerns Greyfriars Bobby, the dog which stayed by his owner's grave for 14 years after he died, becoming a local legend in the process and receiving many treats from visitors who came to look after him. More menacing is the Mackenzie Poltergeist, linked to the tomb of George Mackenzie. People claim to have been pushed over, scratched and bitten near this distinctive tomb of George 'Bloody' Mackenzie, who was Lord Advocate for Scotland during the reign of Charles I (1625–49).

This is a fun tour, with just the right mix of fear and frivolity to keep you on edge and entertained. But it may surprise you to learn that one of Edinburgh's haunted hangouts is on this very bus! Some folk have given feedback about shadowy figures and even a 'phantom passenger'. Chilling stuff!

If you enjoy the Ghost Bus Tour in Edinburgh, the good news is you can join a thrilling and spooky Routemaster tour in London and York, with different local themes to match.

BELOW Taking a ride on this double decker bus is no summer holiday.

DEPARTS FROM OUTSIDE GEORGE IV BRIDGE, EDINBURGH, EH1 1EG
WWW.THEGHOSTBUSTOURS.COM

90 The Arthur's Seat Coffins, Edinburgh

Come face to face with a spooky discovery made on Edinburgh's famous volcanic hill

One of Edinburgh's most popular attractions is Arthur's Seat, a beautiful volcanic hill that rises close to the Old Town and makes for a cracking hike from the Royal Mile. It's not too bad a climb if you're feeling energetic on your spooky Scottish trip. During the summer months, hundreds of tourists can be seen making the pilgrimage to the trig point at the summit. But when a group of boys were on those slopes in June 1836, they discovered something a lot stranger than a good view and a rush of endorphins. They were hunting rabbits for their supper when they found themselves in the entrance to a small cave. Lurking there, behind three slabs of slate, they made the disturbing discovery of 17 miniature coffins. Eight of them still survive and are on display today in the National Museum of Scotland. They still prove to be one of the most intriguing and thought-provoking exhibits in the collection.

Each of the mysterious coffins measures less than 10cm (3.9in) and, even more creepy, they each contain a tiny little wooden figure dressed in clothes that were intricately stitched and glued around them. Why were they there? Nobody seemed to know. The odd discovery hit the headlines and theories soon started to fly around. One of the most widespread was that witchcraft was behind it all. The little 'dolls' were incarnations of the people the witches wanted to inflict harm upon, the rumours insisted. Others suggested the effigies were buried to symbolise loved ones who had died abroad, or maybe they were a superstitious way to look after sailors who had gone to sea. Another train of

ABOVE The area where the dolls were found is extremely atmospheric.
OPPOSITE The rocky summit of Arthur's Seat.

thought is that they were a link to the 17 victims of Burke and Hare, the murderers who had terrorised the city's streets a few years earlier (page 190).

Analysis of the dolls at the University of Edinburgh in 1990 shed some light on what was a very confusing picture. The figures, they discovered, were all made by the same person, although there could be two workers responsible for the coffins. The tools used suggest the coffins could have been the work of a shoemaker. The figures all had their eyes open, so it's unlikely they were made to be corpses in a coffin; one suggestion is that they started out life as toy soldiers. The fabric they are dressed in dates to the early 1830s so they hadn't been in there for long before they were found, and some of them had their arms removed to get them into the coffin. Sadly, some were thought to have been destroyed by the boys who found them, but this is still a significant collection at the museum.

I guess we may never know what the original purpose of these fascinating little figures was, whether it was a sinister form of witchcraft intent on causing harm or a more innocent way of generating a talisman to keep safe those out at sea. Whatever the reason for their existence, anybody who stands in front of this strange discovery is likely to feel a spooky chill in their bones as they gaze into those soulless eyes.

You'll find them on Level 4 of the Scotland Galleries, and you can head up to where they were found on the path to Arthur's Seat that sets off opposite Holyrood Park.

CHAMBERS ST, EDINBURGH, EH1 1JF
WWW.NMS.AC.UK

91 Scotland's Secret Bunker, nr St Andrews, Fife

Walk the underground corridors designed to house Scottish government officials during a nuclear war

Growing up in the 1980s during the tail-end of the Cold War would have been much less fun after watching the film *Threads*. The chilling sci-fi drama, released in 1984, depicted the lead-up to a nuclear war with the Soviet Union, the inevitable destruction of a British city and the ensuing breakdown of society. The scenes never leave anyone who sees it.

During this time of political uncertainty, the threat of war was so serious that a number of subterranean nuclear bunkers were constructed in the hope that military and political officials would still be able to run the country from deep underground. When the Cold War came to an end with the Fall of the Berlin Wall in 1989, many of the bunkers fell into disrepair and some were given a new lease of life as tourist attractions.

Scotland's nuclear bunker is no longer 'secret' – there are plenty of brown tourist signs pointing you in the right direction – and it is one of the spookiest ways to spend an afternoon.

From the surface, it looks like nothing special. Disguised as a farmhouse in rolling countryside, there is another world inside once

BELOW Going underground: the bunker is a creepy, eerie subterranean space.

RIGHT Outside the bunker, before you enter the once secret underground lair.

you proceed beyond the blast doors and head down the slope to the fortress contained within. This is RAF Troywood, a 2,230 sq. m (24,000 sq. ft) command centre built in 1953 and housing planning rooms, dormitories and a mess. Encased in 4.6m (15ft) of reinforced concrete and built over two levels, the hope was that in the event of a nuclear attack some kind of order could be maintained from here. Maybe a military response could be co-ordinated beneath this remote Scottish corner. As you walk down the chilling corridors and look inside the well-maintained rooms, spare a thought for what kind of world would be on the surface were this facility actually needed. And therein lies the reason why this is one of the spookiest places in Britain. This is not about poltergeists or ghostly visions; this is about the living horror being faced by millions of people just 30m (100ft) above this emergency provision for the elite. Some would be allowed shelter, but the likes of you and I would have to stay on the surface. Even those inside would have had to emerge at some point. And emerge to what?

The rooms hidden beneath the Scottish farmhouse were designed to hold 300 people and remain fully operational for a few months after the war started. Peer into the radio rooms and learn how the bunker would have dealt with waste and provided fresh water. Every part of this fascinating place contains what would have been state-of-the-art equipment at the height of the Cold War, but it now seems woefully antiquated, leaving you questioning just what would have been achieved here in reality. Information displayed in this fascinating nuclear bunker details the county's plans in the event of war, including instructions to households about what to do in the worst-case scenario. It all seems so primitive and hopelessly pointless.

A journey down into these depths is a trip back to a time when the world was well and truly at a crossroads. These facilities were built because the threat of nuclear Armageddon was very real. Fortunately, the bunker was never needed. But knowing this secret location even existed, realising the extent to which the plans were developed, it all shows how close the world came to disaster. And considering that alternative future, here at the control centre, is one of the most chilling things I've ever done.

TROYWOOD NR ST ANDREWS, FIFE, KY16 8QH
WWW.SECRETBUNKER.CO.UK

92 Inveraray Jail, Argyll and Bute

Explore this atmospheric Victorian prison, where many say you'll enjoy ghostly company during your visit

Sitting on the banks of Loch Fyne with Scottish mountains rising in the distance, Inveraray Jail is in an idyllic location, in stark contrast to the dreadful events that took place here. In the 19th century, Inveraray Jail was a courthouse and prison. Today, it's open as a museum, giving visitors the chance to glimpse inside the harsh world of Victorian justice and the gruesome torture methods used centuries ago. The folk who work here are quite open about the building's haunted reputation. The sightings have been so significant, many ghost hunters have flocked here in the hope of getting a piece of the action themselves. Plenty of them have not left disappointed.

The building itself is superbly atmospheric and conjures up the perfect supernatural scenario. Thick stone walls and black iron bars contribute to the setting and if you're lucky there'll be a spooky mist hovering over the loch. Things continue to be eerie inside; waxwork figures recreate a courtroom scene where rough justice is being

BELOW The jail is so notorious it has appeared on TV ghost hunts.

handed out, and your guides are dressed as Victorian prison warders. Learn about the cell conditions in the Victorian era and see the tools used to torture people in centuries past. It's guaranteed to make you wince. You can also venture into some of the cells to experience – if only briefly – the conditions in there.

Stepping back in time to discover more about crime and punishment in a harsher society is spine-tingling enough, but what if you're being watched by a ghostly presence throughout? That's what some visitors to Inverary Jail, a place with a formidable reputation amongst spirit hunters, have reported. Shadowy figures have been seen drifting through the corridors and voices heard in empty rooms. One employee said they regularly see somebody crossing from the washroom to the dayroom in the old prison. A number of people imprisoned here died before they could be released and experience freedom again; faint footsteps are occasionally heard – and dismembered voices, too. Several people claim to have felt a presence in the prison, an unexplained and very strong feeling that they are being watched by somebody standing close to them. Children on tours around the prison have been seen crouching in cells talking to an 'old lady' nobody else can see. And then there's the ghost of the angry guard who is said to create an oppressive presence on the upper floors.

The jail is regularly used by paranormal experts for ghost hunts and has featured on TV's *Most Haunted*. Many consider it to be one of the most haunted buildings in Scotland. There have certainly been lots of incidents that are difficult to explain away.

To cement your visit as an unforgettable experience, there's an Escape Room challenge that will test your wits as you try to break out of the prison – something the sorriest inhabitants of this jail could only ever dream of...

CHURCH SQUARE, INVERARAY, PA32 8TX
WWW.INVERARAYJAIL.CO.UK

93 Glencoe, Scottish Highlands

Put on your walking boots and take to the mountain trails in this scenic valley still haunted by a 17th-century tragedy

Glencoe is one of the most peaceful and attractive places on the planet. A bald statement, but I'll hear nothing to convince me otherwise. It's the scene of outstanding beauty; a lush-green, remote haven for hikers, with stunning nature and awesome landforms coming thick and fast as you negotiate the roads, tracks and paths. Red deer can be seen on the hills and golden eagles in the skies. When the sun is shining on Glencoe, it's a photographer's paradise. But even when there is a Scottish mist rolling in and the rain starts falling, this is still an inspirational valley. It brings a new joy with every dawn. No wonder it's attracted hundreds of artists down the centuries, from poets to painters, novelists to

filmmakers. But this serene valley has not always been such a peaceful haven, for it was once filled with terrifying screams during an appalling massacre that haunts the region to this day.

It was on 13 February 1692 when members of the Clan MacDonald were slaughtered in this famous glen on the shocking, merciless orders of King William III (r. 1689–1702). Government soldiers carried out the dreadful attacks, blocking off the top of the valley and beginning the deadly assault from the bottom. Government forces led by the Campbell clan had been given hospitality by Clan MacDonald for the previous two weeks. But early on that February morning, they turned on their hosts in a moment of betrayal that shocked communities across Scotland. Some of the soldiers likely warned the MacDonalds and gave them chance to escape. But many men, women and children were murdered in the cruel attack, while their homes were set on fire. Some historians reckon those who did escape later succumbed to the winter conditions in the mountains. The precise number of those

killed may never be known; some say as many as 38 souls were slain on that tragic morning. And what for? The reason the order was given revolves around an oath of allegiance to the king. The MacDonald clan had taken the oath, but delays in getting messages meant they missed the deadline and were therefore made an example of.

As dusk falls, particularly when the weather is unkind in Glencoe, some people have heard alarmed whispers and chilling cries. Sickening screams have been heard echoing around the hills, while others have claimed to see a kilted Highland spectre, standing solemnly on a hill. Paranormal events appear to be more active on the anniversary of the dreadful massacre, but year-round visitors to this stunning and yet troubled part of the world have claimed to be overcome with an unexplained sorrow. The most alarming claims are those involving a spectral march, a ghostly funeral procession complete with mourners and bagpipes.

Enjoy your visit to Glencoe. Take in the scenery. Leave with your selfies. But spare a thought for the horrors experienced here on that dark February morning.

ABOVE Glencoe is a place of immense beauty but with a very disturbing shadow looming over its history.

THE VISITOR CENTRE IS FOUND AT GLENCOE, BALLACHULISH, PH49 4HX

94 Massacre Cave, Isle of Eigg

Journey to a remote Scottish island, where a terrible mass killing took place in an otherwise peaceful spot by the coast

Board the ferry from Mallaig bound for the Isle of Eigg and you'll soon be sailing across the waves toward an incredible destination. One of the Small Isles of the Inner Hebrides, Eigg sits close to Rum, Cana and Muck, each served by a boat service to the mainland that's generally reliable until the weather starts to throw its stormy dice. Day-trippers come and enjoy a walk around the coast of this remote isle, while more hardcore tourists can arrange to stay over and immerse themselves in isolation over a few days. It's an incredible place, with beautiful views and a genuine desire among the community to have a low carbon footprint by producing green energy. But beyond the tourists smiling for pictures in front of outstanding island scenery there lies a dark, troubled history of fighting clans that once turned this lovely place into a murderous hellhole.

The ferocious feud between Clan MacLeod and Clan MacDonald led to many bitter and bloody encounters. In a time of utter turmoil, hundreds of people died in clashes that were rooted in long-term hatred for each other. This was one of the most severe feuds in history; it makes Shakespeare's famous disagreements between rival families the Montagues and Capulets look like a playground-falling out over Pokémon cards. And one of the most significant, brutal acts was played out in a cave that can be found a short walk away from the ferry terminal.

LEFT The gorgeous setting of Eigg makes the horrendous events here even more shocking.

RIGHT The island's caves provided a doomed hiding place.

Eigg was home to the MacDonalds, while the MacLeods were to be found on the Isle of Skye. In 1577, a group of MacLeods were forced to land on Eigg due to bad weather. Their behaviour incensed the local MacDonalds. Accusations were made about McLeods raping women and killing cattle, while the MacDonalds were said to have killed some of those seeking shelter and sent others away on their ship. The accounts differ wildly depending on which clan is telling the story. But either way, it appears the MacLeods were left bearing one hell of a grudge and set about getting revenge.

Eventually, a group arrived on Eigg looking for trouble. Their arrival had been spotted and most of the MacDonalds decided to hide in the Cave of Francis. The MacLeods saw one of the MacDonalds, though, and were able to follow footprints in the snow that led them to the cave. Once there, legend has it they started a fire at the entrance to the cave. Smoke drifted inside and killed nearly 400 people taking shelter in there. Remains of the bodies were discovered for decades, with most being removed and reburied in 1854.

Today, the Cave of Francis is more widely known as the Massacre Cave, for obvious reasons. The interior has a dark, menacing feel and will leave you with a haunting sense of just how brutal the conflicts between these clans were.

CATCH THE FERRY FROM MALLAIG TO EIGG AND THEN CHECK IN WITH THE VISITOR CENTRE TO MAKE SURE YOU'RE ON THE RIGHT PATH
WWW.ISLEOFEIGG.ORG

95 Loch Ness, Drumnadrochit, Highland

Keep a watchful eye as you sail across the gentle waters of Loch Ness, and you might just spot the legendary Nessie herself

The boat moved gracefully across the water, a calm peace descending over us that seemed equally fuelled by the distance from the shore and the majestic mountains of the Scottish Highlands. The very mention of the name 'Loch Ness' conjures up an image of a fearsome marine creature, or at least the grainy black and white images that claim to have captured this world-famous beast. I've watched documentaries about it, enjoyed *The Family Ness* cartoon on TV as a kid and, along with my children, watched the *Scooby Doo* gang have an adventure in the area. But despite the folklore, I'd always known it wasn't real. Right? I'd been guided by my head to believe that surely there would be more evidence in the public domain were Nessie to actually exist...

And yet once you're out on these waters, once you're scanning the horizon for every ripple, there's more than an element of doubt that creeps in. You end up *wanting* to be the person who sees her, who captures an image and later tells the tale in the pub (a tale that is no doubt labelled a hoax by all and sundry). You *want* to see it, so you scan the blue horizon as keenly as a smartphone reads a QR code. And while you do look out over the side of the boat, there's a sudden, spooky unease that grips you. What if there actually is an enormous prehistoric plesiosaur swimming below your vessel?

If you're looking for spooky, otherworldly experiences in the UK (and I presume you are, given you're this far into the book), then going onto the waters of Loch Ness is essential. I'm not talking about standing on the

RIGHT The Loch Ness Monster: can it be real?
BELOW The sensational setting of Loch Ness.

shores and looking out across the water; you've got to be bobbing about on a boat to reach the full levels of creepiness. Drumnadrochit is the place to head to, as this is where you'll find the Loch Ness Centre and an immersive tour through 500 million years of history. Between March and November there are also hourly cruises on the loch led by an expert skipper with extensive knowledge of the waters and the legends within. They'll also have a hydrophone on hand to listen out for creatures of the deep.

Sightings of Nessie date back to the 6th century, but it was in 1933 that local hotelier Aldie Mackay really sparked things off. She ran the Drumnadrochit Hotel – now the visitor centre – and glimpsed a whale-like creature rising from the water. It created huge waves in its wake, and not just in the water; when word got around of the sighting, the tourists flooded in. Other sightings and photographs soon appeared in the press and the legend of Nessie was secured. And whether you believe or not, you cannot help but scour the horizon for a ripple or two.

For the full experience, come here over 'the Quest' weekend, during which visitors can become Nessie Hunters as part of a 'surface watch' and enjoy talks from a range of experts.

LOCH VISITOR CENTRE,
DRUMNADROCHIT, IV63 6AN
WWW.LOCHNESS.COM

96 Culloden Battle Site, nr Inverness, Highland

Spend the day at the informative visitor centre and walk around the battle site, where spirits from that historic fight are still said to roam

The spring of 1746 was a tumultuous time in British history and the battle for power. The Jacobite army had previously attempted a march on London and got as far as Derby before turning back for Scotland. They faced a showdown in Scotland against the advancing government soldiers led by the Duke of Cumberland. The Jacobite army was being rallied by Prince Charles, who wanted a Stuart king and aimed to stop the English taking Inverness. It was a delicately poised conflict that divided communities and even households. The crunch point came at Culloden on 16 April.

Close to 1pm, the Jacobites fired on the government soldiers and received a barrage of cannon shot. When the feared Highland charge was ordered, the government troops were well prepared with their gunfire and bayonets. The battle lasted barely an hour. It cost the lives of 1,300 men, 1,250 of them Jacobites. The one-sided rout saw the Duke of Cumberland emerge victorious, shifting the power balance in the Highlands for ever. With so much pain and misery inflicted on men in this

ABOVE The place where the English soldiers were buried.
OPPOSITE Culloden was a key moment in British history, but there are still many mysteries surrounding it.

otherwise gloriously beautiful landscape, the remote field of the battle has become a memorial with a very informative visitor centre filling in any historical gaps you may have. So many souls were lost, there are inevitably ghostly tales passed down the generations.

The ghosts of the fallen soldiers are said to rise again on the anniversary of the battle and there have been several reports of a tall man in Highland dress roaming the scene. He has even been heard to mutter the word 'defeated'. A woman in 1936 told of her walk across the battlefield, and lifting a piece of tartan cloth to discover the apparition of a wounded Scottish soldier underneath it. And hers is not the only sorry story of disturbed and gruesome Jacobites lingering on long after the battle's o'er. The sounds of the fighting have been heard by many a visitor, the wind whistling and bringing with it the clanking of metal and the moans of the injured. Heard most frequently at dawn and at dusk, it's as if the suffering of that fateful day has been trapped in time and those who fell are unable to escape the violence.

Standing on the Culloden battle site, you get an enormous sense of history. This is a place not only where many people lost their lives but also where the nation came to a key junction and its future fate was decided. A different outcome could have had ramifications that continued to this very day. And so the sense of loss surrounding Culloden goes beyond the death and suffering to include the deterioration of an idea, a movement. To that end, many visitors treading in the footsteps of the soldiers report an overwhelming feeling of melancholy, a deep sadness. Some say they have been watched on the battle site. Many come away with a level of grief they were not anticipating. A ghostly figure – perhaps from the time or maybe from later decades – is sometimes heard on the moor crying over the fallen Jacobites. The sorrow is not reserved for those still living.

CULLODEN BATTLEFIELD, INVERNESS, IV2 5EU
WWW.NTS.ORG.UK/VISIT/PLACES/CULLODEN

97
98
99
Cardiff
100
97 Beaumaris Castle and Gaol, Anglesey
98 Carew Castle, nr Tenby, Pembrokeshire
99 The Skirrid Inn, Llanvihangel, Monmouthshire
100 Cardiff Castle, Glamorgan

Wales

97 Beaumaris Castle and Gaol, Anglesey

Beaumaris, on the north coast of the pretty island of Anglesey, is home to more than its fair share of hauntings...

On the face of it, this impressive, moated castle with formidable towers and turrets is one of the best-preserved ruined fortresses in Wales. But the truth is that this castle on the Anglesey coast was never actually finished. In a tale that could come straight from the 21st century, they ran out of money, pulled the funding and abandoned it half finished. It was the work of Edward I (r. 1272–1307), who had already spent a great deal of time and money fortifying the north coast of Wales. Great castles at Conwy, Caernarfon and Harlech had already been completed and the plan for Beaumaris was to create the finest castle of them all. But with funds running low and skirmishes with the Scots taking up many resources, the project was put on hold in the 1320s and never completed. By that time, it was already a huge, impressive and almost perfectly symmetrical castle. There was a water-filled moat with its own dock, 300 arrow loops in the outer walls and inner defences made up of four concentric rings. Six great towers were partially finished, as was the huge Llanfaes Gate. Beaumaris Castle proudly makes up part of the Gwynedd World Heritage Site, putting it on the same scale as global

BELOW This formidable fortress is said to be home to many restless spirits.

ABOVE The towers are part of a UNESCO World Heritage Site.
BELOW The statue of Edward I.

treasures such as Rome's Colosseum and the Great Wall of China. And it's also home to some terrifying tales.

Despite never being finished, Beaumaris Castle was still active. It was besieged by the Welsh in 1403 and retaken by English forces a couple of years later. During the Civil War, it was used to support the Royalists before falling to Parliamentarians. A Welsh Catholic priest was held in the dungeons and then executed here in the 16th century. Plenty of unhappy folk have passed through the castle over the centuries, and so there are many restless souls still hanging around, according to paranormal experts who have spent time here. But unlike many of its contemporary castles, the ghosts associated with Beaumaris cannot be easily linked to individuals. They're more nameless spirits, perhaps belonging to the thousands of workers who built this grand structure, or maybe the soldiers who were once stationed here. But whoever they are, they have been responsible for some pretty wild and recurring phenomena.

The restless spirits of Beaumaris have been experienced in different parts of the castle. Visitors have mentioned feeling

the temperature suddenly drop and the strangest feelings of being watched as they walk around the centuries-old ruin. Footsteps have also been heard in all parts of the castle, heavy and foreboding. Perhaps this is the timeless sound of soldiers on the march, or the thuds of the labourers transporting the heavy stones.

But the hotspot for hauntings has to be the castle chapel. You'll be brave to venture in there, particularly if you're on your own or few other visitors are around. It's a peaceful place, perfect for a moment of solitude and reflection. But imagine being here and listening in shock as the room filled with the sound of long-dead monks saying prayers and joining in collective chants. The room returns to quiet soon after, but several people have reported having this chilling experience.

While in Beaumaris, save time to visit the gaol. It's another spooky place, filled with a heartbreaking atmosphere. Built in 1829 to house 30 prisoners, those incarcerated here had to deal with the whipping room, solitary confinement

and a treadmill (a punishment device with continuously rotating steps, and the forerunner to the modern fitness machine). At least two men were hanged here and the gibbet (cage) is on display. One of those to be executed was Richard Rowlands who killed his father-in-law in 1862. He argued his innocence right to the end and, legend has it, put a curse on the gaol's clock. If he is innocent, he decreed, the clock would forever show the wrong time. And, despite repairs, it has...

YOU'LL FIND THE CASTLE AT CASTLE STREET, BEAUMARIS, LL58 8AP, AND THE GAOL AT STEEPLE LANE, BEAUMARIS, LL58 8EP
WWW.CADW.GOV.WALES/VISIT/PLACES-TO-VISIT/BEAUMARIS-CASTLE AND WWW.VISITANGLESEY.CO.UK/EN-GB/EXPLORE/BEAUMARIS-GAOL

BELOW There also stunning views to be had towards the mainland when you visit Beaumaris.

98 Carew Castle, nr Tenby, Pembrokeshire

Enjoy an afternoon at this historic castle and mill in south Wales, where there's always a chance of seeing a ghost or two

Today it's an impressive-looking fortress standing ruinous on the banks of the Carew River, but this much-loved castle has a history stretching back to the Norman invasion, having first been established here in the late 11th century. Additional fortifications were added in the following centuries, until Carew was transformed from a medieval fortress into an Elizabethan manor. A mill was established alongside, often referred to as the 'French Mill' because of the French burr stones used in its construction. This is the only tidal mill in Wales to have been restored – one of only five in the UK – and while it is no longer working, the machinery once used here is still intact. Carew Castle, then, is a great way to learn about the history of this part of Wales. As ever, though, some of that history was tragic, and there are spirits from the past that are said to linger here and make an appearance before lucky (or not-so-lucky) visitors.

Carew Castle is home to not one but two famous ghostly legends, and they are polar opposites. The first tells of a beautiful young woman, Princess Nest, the daughter of the King of Deheubarth, and once said to be the prettiest woman in Wales. She was raised in the court of Henry I (r. 1100–1135) and became his mistress, bearing his illegitimate child. Nest was married off to Gerald de Windsor and the couple moved into Carew Castle. They grew to love each other, but her cousin, Owain, was overcome by Nest's beauty and kidnapped her in a raid around 1109. She was held at his Cilgerran Castle for six years, where she had further children before being rescued. The princess was married again when Gerald died, but her heart remained in Carew Castle, and this is thought to be the reason why her soul still patrols the grounds. Sightings are more common than you might think and many local folk have their own stories about spotting the ghost of this beautiful Welsh princess. She's often seen looking out towards the river, with

a mournful and melancholy expression.

The second ghostly legend is much more unusual – it features a Barbary ape that has a penchant for returning to its home on stormy nights. But how on Earth did a Barbary ape make its way to south Wales in the first place? Naturally, it was all down to the wealthy and well-travelled man who lived here, Sir Roland Rhys. In the 17th century, he brought back an injured ape he had rescued from a shipwrecked Spanish galleon. Why it was on the ship is another matter. But the ape, which he named Satan, came back with him to Wales and was trained to respond to a series of whistles, and kept almost as a jester. All very normal so far, then.

But things took a dark turn one night when Sir Roland ended up in an argument with a merchant called Horwitz, after their children ran away with each other. Legend has it that Sir Roland was so angry, he released Satan from his chains and ordered him to kill Horwitz, who was badly injured in the scrap that followed. But it was Sir Roland who was discovered dead the morning after, lying in a pool of blood, with the ape nowhere to be seen – though some versions of the tale say Satan also died in the brawl. Whatever happened on that stormy night – and much is still shrouded in mystery – it was a traumatic event for those who apparently witnessed it, including the servants.

However, if you're visiting this site on a stormy night, make sure you keep watch for Satan's spectre, and listen for the growls and scratching noises that have also been heard around the castle.

CAREW, NR TENBY, PEMBROKESHIRE, SA70 8SL
WWW.PEMBROKESHIRECOAST.WALES/CAREW-CASTLE

BELOW There are two ghostly legends at Carew Castle if you dare to investigate.

99 The Skirrid Inn, Llanvihangel, Monmouthshire

Try to make contact with felons executed for petty crimes at what's claimed to be the most haunted pub in Wales

Nestling in the shadow of the beautiful Ysgyryd Fawr (Skirrid mountain), you'll find what some believe to be the most haunted pub in Wales, beckoning you in with its good ale and even better stories. Just over the border in Monmouthshire, the Skirrid Inn is a popular place for people to enjoy a pub meal – but you're unlikely to be alone in the bar, according to many ghost hunters. In this very pub, you'll be chilled to know that there's a wooden beam once used to hang felons from the surrounding area. It's a claim I'm sure can't be matched by your local. Over 180 people met their end in this building, swinging from the beam, and it's thought that several of their spirits still loiter about after-hours. So why here? Well, this watering hole has been here for 900 years, but as well as providing pints of ale it also used to serve up some rough justice. The Skirrid Inn, you see, doubled up as a courthouse in medieval times, overseen by a law enforcer ominously known as the 'Hanging Judge'. That's really going to put you off being put on trial here, isn't it? Judge George Jeffreys was known for punishing petty perpetrators with the noose for crimes as minor as stealing a sheep. And, today, patrons have reported seeing hanging ghosts in the bar, and also feeling their necks tighten. Some claim to have rope marks around their neck for some time after the

LEFT Many people were hanged in this very building.

ABOVE The Skirrid is notoriously haunted and a destination for serious ghost hunters.

terrifying ordeal. Are these events caused by the spirits of those executed in this lovely Welsh hostelry?

The spooks here aren't all guilty of crimes, however. Fanny Price worked as a landlady here, and guests claim to have heard her footsteps and even smelt her perfume. Though her ghost has never been seen, you can visit her grave in the local churchyard.

So many spirits are said to haunt this mountain inn and its history is so long and troubled that it's captured the interest of many a ghost hunter. Rather than shying away from the horrible happenings or trying to keep them quiet, fearful it may put off potential patrons, the pub has embraced the spooky side of things with gusto and now hosts regular ghost-hunting evenings. You can sign up with the ghost hunters at www.hauntingnights.co.uk and enjoy a meal at the pub before hunting for evidence of the hauntings. The event known as the Spooky Sunday Ghost Hunt is not for the faint-hearted. Not at all. During this two-hour ghostly experience you can expect to take part in various methods to try and summon the spirits of those hanged on the beam down the centuries. Expect an evening of hands-on ghost hunting using Ouija boards, table tipping, glass divination and psychic seances, as well as modern-day ghost hunting techniques. You have to be over the age of 16 to take part, and under-18s need to be accompanied by an adult. Approach the evening with an open mind and be ready for the odd shock; not all the spirits in this rural Welsh pub come in 25ml servings.

LLANVIHANGEL CRUCORNEY, ABERGAVENNY, MONMOUTHSHIRE, NP7 8DH
WWW.HAUNTINGNIGHTS.CO.UK

100 Cardiff Castle, Glamorgan

The historic fortress stands right in the centre of the Welsh capital and is a hotbed for fans of history – and hauntings

Conveniently located right in the heart of Cardiff, the capital city's castle has a history stretching back more than 2,000 years. Romans, Normans, soldiers and civilians sheltering from the Blitz have all made use of this site that now sits in the midst of shops and cafés in the bustling city centre. Go beyond the walls of the castle and you'll be treated to some classic sights, not least the Norman keep and the clock tower. The first fort was built here by the Romans around AD 50 with the aim of keeping the local Silures tribe in order. One Roman fort was built out of stone, and the remains of one of its walls can be seen today in the visitor centre.

After the Norman invasion, further fortification took place, and throughout the centuries the castle as we know it took shape and was passed from noble family to noble family. In 1766, it came into the possession of the Bute family, and by the 1860s, John Crichton-Stuart, 3rd Marquess of Bute, was thought to be the richest man not only in Wales but in the entire world.

During the Second World War, the castle took on an important role for the city's population when old underground tunnels were opened up and used as bomb shelters. With so much history, Cardiff Castle clearly has a tale or two to tell. And some of them definitely fall into the paranormal.

One of the most oft-sighted ghosts roaming amid the castle walls belongs to John Crichton-Stuart, 2nd Marquess of Bute (who upon his death left his vast wealth to his son, the aforementioned 3rd Marquess). He was an important figure in Cardiff and played a crucial role in turning the city into a major coal-exporting port. In 1848, he died suddenly in a chamber behind the library. It appears he could not let go of his family home and decided to hang around for a few more centuries, as his apparition has been spotted several times standing by the fireplace in the library. The Marquess will sometimes turn and float right through a 1.8m (6ft) thick wall, which seems a bit wild. But it all starts to make a little more sense when you find out this part of the room is said to have had a door when he was alive.

BELOW The huge castle walls are a key attraction in Cardiff city centre.

Witnesses have also reported the spirit is a tall man wearing a red cloak. Spookily, this matches the image of the Marquess in one of the castle's eerie portraits that still hangs here. The most famous sighting came in 1976 when visitors mentioned a tall man in a red cloak actually pushing past them. The figure scowled at the people in his home, then vanished.

More apparitions of ghosts have been seen in and around this fabulous castle, one of the more notable being a faceless figure in a grey skirt. Spotted near the chapel, this one is believed to be of a more mischievous nature and has been known to move objects around the castle. The posthumous japester has been joined by other female ghosts, including one gliding by the adjacent river and signalling towards the thick, stone walls.

There's practically a ghostly tale in every corner of Cardiff Castle, and that's not surprising when you learn of the history that oozes from every wall. There's a female haunting the clock tower, a ghostly soldier once stationed here is said to still be on patrol, while there is talk of doors opening and closing on their own in the middle of the night. And let's not forget the 19th-century tales of a phantom coach and horses clattering into the courtyard. Hooves stomped, wheels pounded and bells rang out, but when those who heard it went to investigate ... nothing! I'm sure you'll return home from your own trip unscathed, though. Probably.

ABOVE The castle keep has overseen many spectral sightings.
OPPOSITE The clock tower is said to be home to a female ghost.

CASTLE STREET, CARDIFF, CF10 3RB
WWW.CARDIFFCASTLE.COM

Index

Photo Credits

All photos are the property of the author with the exception of:

Alnwick Garden: 170–1
Bloody Tour of York: 134
Bodmin Jail: 17, 18
Cardiff Council: 218–19, 220, 221
Carew Castle: 208–9, 214–15
Chapter of Canterbury Cathedral: 42, 43
Chillingham Castle: 173
Clink Prison Museum: 52t, 52b
Coffin Works: 90, 91
Creative Commons: 14 (Mark Fosh), 19 (Robert Linsdell), 21 (Markles55), 23 (Dave Morton), 30–1 (Mark Longair), 38–9 (Chris Jefferson), 46 (Tim Sheerman-Chase), 50 (Flowcomm), 51 (Heather Smithers), 72–3 (Martin V Morris), 77 (Liza31337), 85 (John W Schulze), 92–93 (Andy Sim), 94 (Catherine Poh Huay Tan), 97 (Amanda Slater), 106–7, 107t (Glen Bowman), 108t (Matt Brown), 135 (Ray in Manila), 144t (Dun Deagh), 144b (Amanda Slater), 174–5 (Richard Whitaker), 176–7 (Chris Fleming), 180–1 (RJ Photos UK), 184–5 (Gary Campbell-Hall), 186–7 (Petr Meissner), 194 (gnomonic), 195 (Rob Schulze), 204–5 (Peter Mulligan)
Creswell Crags Heritage Trust: 112, 113
Dorchester Prison: 24l, 24r
Getty: 88, 89
Ghost Bus Tours Edinburgh: 193
Gloucester Prison: 82
Gordon Young: 169
Greene King: 104–5
Hack Green Secret Nuclear Bunker: 100, 101
Haunted Haworth: 133
Inverary Jail: 198
iStock: 2–3, 8, 10–11, 12–13, 16, 26–7, 32, 34–5, 36–7, 64–5, 71, 74–5, 95, 108–9, 110–11, 120–1, 140–1, 155, 161, 163, 172, 178–9, 200–1, 206, 207, 216, 217
Jennifer Walker: 142
Kelvedon Hatch Secret Nuclear Bunker: 70
Liz Fox: 129
Loch Ness Centre: 204t
Madame Tussauds: 63
Manchester Museum, The University of Manchester: 128 (Paul Cliff)
Mercat Tours: 188
National Justice Museum: 102
Nick Mailer Photography: 154, 189
North Yorkshire Council: 159 (Tom Arber)
Oxford Castle and Prison: 78, 79
Real Mary King's Close: 191, 192
Rob Marks: 39r
Royal Shakespeare Company: 83 (Manuel Harlan), 84 (Marc Brenner)
Samlesbury Hall: 152
Scotland's Secret Bunker: 196, 197
Shepton Mallet Prison: 28, 29
Shiverpool Tours: 124
Shrewsbury Prison: 98, 99
Smart Banda: 114
St Dunstan in the East: 55
St Leonard's Church: 40, 41
Visit Britain: 44–5 (Robert McConkey), 48–9, 86–7 (Robin Creative Media), 160 (Simon Palmer), 183
Visit Wales: 210, 211t, 211b, 212–13
York Ghost Merchants: 139, 140l